T0113936

The Apostolic Doctrine

A Biblical Guide for
New Believers

ROBERTO TINOCO

WESTBOW
PRESS®
A DIVISION OF THOMAS NELSON
& ZONDERVAN

WestBow Press books may be ordered through booksellers or by contacting:

WestBow Press
A Division of Thomas Nelson & Zondervan
1663 Liberty Drive
Bloomington, IN 47403
www.westbowpress.com
844-714-3454

Scripture taken from the King James Version of the Bible.

ISBN: 978-1-6642-5393-3 (sc)
ISBN: 978-1-6642-5395-7 (hc)
ISBN: 978-1-6642-5394-0 (e)

Library of Congress Control Number: 2021925649

Print information available on the last page.

WestBow Press rev. date: 01/12/2022

Acknowledgments

I want to deeply appreciate the unconditional support of my family in this project. My wife Normita, my Daughter Becky and her husband Augusto; my Son Alex and his wife Marissa and my Son Bobby and his wife Luz because they are my greatest inspiration after God. I also want to thank Sister Ana Arciniega for helping with the translation of this book and Sister Jessica Rojas for the editing work she did. Many thanks to both of you for the excellent work.

Presentation

The Doctrine is perhaps one of the most important teachings in the life of every Christian who wants to follow Christ. Also, for those who want to nourish themselves with the knowledge of the word of God and the teaching that is to lead him to a different life in Christ Jesus. In addition, it is very important to know it because it tells us what we believe as a church concerning the most important doctrinal topics in the Bible. Among them, those who are indispensable to eternal life.

Knowing the doctrine is important, because it determines the basis of our theological position, what we believe about God and of God, in front of other creeds. In addition, the doctrine determines the way we are to develop in the life and how we will live our Christianity. In other words, the way we conduct ourselves reveals the kind of doctrine we have. A Christian who is founded on solid doctrine will lead a life that pleases God, will not fall so easy, let alone be carried by any wind of doctrine (Ephesians 4:14) but is to remain in the ways of God.

The book "The Apostolic Doctrine" will teach the reader how God wants us to live the Christian life as children of God. In this book we will learn about the basic and fundamental themes of Christian doctrine, written in a simple way, in a common language and within the reach of those who are just beginning the Christian career, as well as those who want to enrich their knowledge. Also, "The Apostolic Doctrine" book can serve as a training tool for all those, leaders, teachers, and educators engaged in the preparation and training of new believers.

Dr. Roberto Tinoco December 2021

Contents

Tables

Chapter 1

Introduction to the Apostolic Doctrine

≈

And he came down to Capernaum, a city of Galilee, and taught them on the sabbath days. And they were astonished at his doctrine: for his word was with power.

Luke 4:31-32

The teaching of the doctrine is the most important thing for a Christian, especially when the Christian life begins. When a person comes to Christ, one of the most indispensable things for his or her spiritual journey, is undoubtedly the knowledge of faith – in other words, what one believes in. If people do not know the basic points of their doctrine, they will be easy prey to any misguided teaching. Therefore, in this chapter, we will learn about the meaning of the word doctrine, what apostolic doctrine is, the teaching of Jesus and His apostles, as well as the importance of doctrine in the life of a child of God.

Definition

When we talk about doctrine, we should ask ourselves, "What is doctrine? What does it mean? Also, what is the effect of doctrine in the life of a child of God?"

To begin with, in the Bible itself we find some definitions of this word. For example, in the Old Testament, the word doctrine, is translated from the Hebrew word shemua and means, "what is received." In the

New Testament, the word used is didaché, which means "teaching; what is taught; the act of giving some instruction." Taking these words into consideration, we can affirm that doctrine is a teaching or instruction that is taught or received.[1]

When people refer to the doctrine of a Christian, they usually refer to what and how a person believes in a certain topic related to his or her faith and how to teach on it. In some Christian circles, it is also known as religious tradition. Finally, the doctrine has a powerful impact on the life of the believer because it determines how the believer is to serve God and how to live.

The Apostolic Doctrine

Many times, we have heard about "the apostolic doctrine", but what is it? In a simple answer, we can say that apostolic doctrine is the teaching given or received according to the teachings of Christ and the apostles of the Lord. It is the teaching that Christ and his apostles taught their followers.

We, as a Christian church must follow the doctrine of Christ and his apostles as taught by the very word of God.

> And are built upon the foundation of the apostles and prophets, Jesus Christ himself being the chief corner stone. Ephesians 2:20

Based on this scripture, we must focus our study on the teachings of Christ and the apostles.

---

[1] W. E. Vine, Diccionario Expositivo en Enciclopedia Electrónica Ilumina, (Orlando, FL. Caribe-Betania, 2005).

The Doctrine of Christ

When Christ came into this world, He dedicated himself to preaching the word of God, and all the words He said were his doctrine or teaching. For example, Matthew counts an episode where what we are saying is manifested:

> And it came to pass, when Jesus had ended these sayings, the people were astonished at his doctrine: For he taught them as one having authority, and not as the scribes. Matthew 7:28–29

In this text, we can see the difference between the teachings of Christ and the teachings of the contemporary religious leaders. The Lord spoke to them a different word and taught them with authority. Here we can notice two things:

1. It's a true teaching.
   Jesus's teaching included the complete truth of God. One should not take part of the Bible alone, but every doctrine must be in harmony with the rest of the scripture. The scribes and Pharisees taught only what was right for them, and often their teachings were of men and far from the truth, so Christ criticized them strongly (Mark 7:7–9). It is precisely these types of teachings that must be exposed – the many false doctrines that have emerged to form religions on a single verse of scripture or only a part that suits them.

2. It is a teaching with authority.
   Another thing that differentiated the doctrine of Christ from that of the religious of his day was authority. The authority Jesus spoke to was not only because he was the Christ, but also because his actions supported what He said – unlike the religious, who spoke the Law of God, but did not practice what they preached (Matthew 23:2–3). This last point is so important, for the doctrine is something that marks the life of all who practice it.

It is unfortunate to see people who claim to be Christians to live contrary to what they preach.

The Doctrine of the Apostles

The apostles of Christ received all the teachings of Jesus and taught them to the church. The early church practiced the doctrine of Christ and the apostles. The biblical text reads:

> And they continued steadfastly in the apostles' doctrine and fellowship, and in breaking of bread, and in prayers. Acts. 2:42

It was the apostles who continued with all the teachings Jesus gave them intensively. They simply passed them on to the early Christians and thus, made it possible for them to be transmitted today. Apostolic doctrine is a teaching based on what Christ and His apostles preached and lived. If people want to know about true doctrine, they must go to the Bible to see what Christ and the apostles taught.

This book will address fundamental themes of the apostolic faith, such as the Bible; God, Jesus Christ, and the Holy Ghost; humans, their creation and fall; sin; repentance; and how to be saved. In addition, the reader will learn about church practices, such as standards of holiness, tithes and offerings, holy supper, and his or her future with Christ. The child of God will enjoy and build faith with apostolic doctrine.

The Importance of Doctrine in the Believer

Another aspect to consider is the importance of doctrine in the life of the child of God. The doctrine is the most important part of a Christian's life, and it is fundamental to making a difference in the world. Do you remember the religious of Jesus's time? They were called by Jesus bleached tombs (Matthew 23:27) because they taught and exhibited that they served God but were not really practicing what they preached.

Those who have true doctrine and practice must make a difference in this world. The doctrine must change us in every way, from the way we think, to the way we speak, and above all, it must lead us in this world. The doctrine is the most important part of the Christian life.

Furthermore, the doctrine is also a matter of survival in God's way. A person who lives according to the doctrine will be a person who endures in the ways of the Lord and will not be moved by anything. The Lord Jesus uses the example of two houses that are shaken by various situations to try to bring them down; one is built on the rock and another on the sand. Let's see what happens:

> Therefore, whosoever heareth these sayings of mine, and doeth them, I will liken him unto a wise man, which built his house upon a rock: And the rain descended, and the floods came, and the winds blew, and beat upon that house; and it fell not: for it was founded upon a rock. And everyone that heareth these sayings of mine, and doeth them not, shall be likened unto a foolish man, which built his house upon the sand: And the rain descended, and the floods came, and the winds blew, and beat upon that house; and it fell: and great was the fall of it. And it came to pass, when Jesus had ended these sayings, the people were astonished at his doctrine: For he taught them as one having authority, and not as the scribes. Matthew 7:24–29

In this biblical passage, Jesus emphasizes that the house that was built on the rock is the one that remains before the various kinds of whippings. Being built on the rock means, the one who hears and obeys the word, is the one who stands before the various scourges that arise. On the other hand, those who hear but do not obey are compared to those who build on the sand, they will fall. That's exactly what happens in the Christian life. Only those who build on the rock will prevail. Note that the two houses suffered the same setbacks, but the one with a solid foundation remained. This is what the doctrine is.

In the Christian life, only those who adopt the doctrine will remain essential to their lives. That is why Paul demands from the Ephesians spiritual maturity, so they won't be carried by any wind of doctrine (Ephesians 4:13–14). We have found that many people who convert to Christianity but neglect things as important as their foundation will not remain. The book, "La Deserción en la Iglesia (The Desertion in the Church)," deals with the reasons people abandon the Lord's way; some of the reasons are precisely a lack of knowledge of the doctrine and a poor relationship with God. For that reason, we must emphasize that knowing the doctrine is not enough. A strong relationship with God is also needed.[2]

Conclusion

We conclude this chapter by emphasizing that the doctrine is important in Christianity and a fundamental part in the growth of a child of God. Therefore, it is wise to learn the doctrine and to know it, especially those topics that are fundamental to faith and will make a difference in life. Furthermore, having knowledge of the doctrine will help explain it, when necessary, and prevent a child of God from being dragged by any false doctrines. Additionally, a Christian must know the fundamental themes of his faith and communicate them to his loved ones and friends, for ultimately, that is the goal of every child of God, which is to bear witness to the good news of salvation.

---

[2] Roberto Tinoco, *La Deserción en la Iglesia: Por qué la gente se va y qué podemos hacer*, (Bloomington IN: WestBow Press, 2016), 75.

Chapter 2

The Bible

≈

*And that from a child thou hast known the holy
scriptures, which are able to make thee wise unto
salvation through faith which is in Christ Jesus.*

2 TIMOTHY 3:15

A child of God must base his or her faith on the word of God, namely the
Bible. No one should simply believe in human opinions and concepts.
True Christian doctrine is based on sacred scriptures and not on the
opinions or philosophies of men. The Bible is the most important
book for every Christian as it contains the laws of God and the plan of
salvation for man, among other things. As children of God, we must
love and respect the Bible; and we must know it to be saved and to be
wise.

In this chapter we will learn basic principles from the book so important
to God's children. The Bible contains God's will for our lives. We will
focus on the meaning of the word "Bible". In addition, we will learn how
it was written, how it is organized, and how it has reached us in our time.
We will also learn why we should believe in it and learn practical advice
for reading and studying.

Definition

The Illustrated Biblical dictionary says, "Bible is the name by which the Sacred Scriptures of the Christian church are designated from a very old age". In addition, it reveals that the name "Bible" comes from Greek through Latin and means "The Books".[3] For its part, the illustrated dictionary of the Bible says that the word "Bible" comes from the Greek word biblión, and means "short book"; that is, collection of short books. He adds, "which is the name given to the collection of writings that the Christian church considers divinely inspired." This term was first used in the late 4th century AD. In Greek, "la biblía" was a plural neutral, but when translated to Latin it was attributed the female genus, due to its ending in "a". Hence, our custom in Spanish to refer to "the Bible".[4]

The Bible also receives other names within its pages such as: The Holy Scriptures and the Law of God, but one of the most used is, the Word of God. Ediberto López says that the concept "Word of God" is woven among the many traditions that we find in the Bible. He also states that when Biblical passages are called on God's word to some oracle – a saying of wisdom or account – part of the premise is that something has occurred according to God's will.[5]

The Content and Organization of the Bible

Content

The Bible contains 66 books that form the sacred canon, which the Christian church recognizes as inspired by God. Although there are other versions that have added books to the Bible (i.e., "The Apocryphal and Deuterocanonical Books), the Christian Church recognizes only 66 books as inspired by God.

---

[3] *Nuevo Diccionario Bíblico Ilustrado*, (Terrassa, Barcelona, Editorial CLE 1985).
[4] *Diccionario Ilustrado de la Biblia*, (Nashville TN: Tomas Nelson, 2001), Pg. 309.
[5] Ediberto López-Rodríguez, *Cómo se formó la Biblia*, (Minneapolis, MN: Augsburg Fortress, 2006), pg. 13.

The word canon according to the biblical dictionary comes from the Hebrew word "kaneh" meaning carrizo or cane and is used to always measure in a literal sense. (We can see an example in Ezekiel 40:5.) In addition, it is added that from this symmetrical word comes the Hebrew word "kanon" which the King James Version translates as a rule or norm. When we speak of the canon of the Bible, we refer to the books that were duly measured by the church to belong to the compendium of sacred writings; in other words, the books approved by the Christian Church.[6]

Organization

The Bible contains two main divisions that are: The Old and New Testaments. The Old Testament was written by and to the ancient Hebrews or Jews and is known as the Hebrew Bible. According to Dr. Ediberto López, the Hebrew Bible was organized into 24 books (which are the equivalent of the 39 books of the Christian Bible). The Jews divide these 24 books into three parts that are called the Tanakh; which comes from three Hebrew words, Torah (the law), Nevi'im, (the prophets from Joshua to Malachi), and Ketuvim, (the writings, which includes Psalms; the books of wisdom; Ruth; Esther; the history of the chronicles; and Daniel).[7]

On the other hand, the New Testament was written by and for the church. Unlike the Old Testament, according to Dr. Lopez, all Christians, regardless of the religious tradition share the same books and the same order.[8] Both Testaments are the word of God, or the Bible, for the Christian church. However, it is important to emphasize that the Jews do not have within their Bible the New Christian Testament, because they do not recognize Jesus as the Messiah to come.

The Old Testament contains 39 books which are grouped as follows:

---

[6] *Diccionario Ilustrado de la Biblia*, (Nashville TN: Tomas Nelson, 2001), 362.
[7] Ediberto Lopez, Op. cit. 35.
[8] Ibid. 67.

- Five legislative books: Genesis, Exodus, Leviticus, Numbers and Deuteronomy.
- Twelve historical books: Joshua, Judges, Ruth, 1 and 2 Samuel, 1 and 2 Kings, 1 and 2 Chronicles, Ezra, Nehemiah, and Esther.
- Five poetic books: Job, Psalms, Proverbs, Ecclesiastes, and Songs.
- Seventeen prophetic books: Five Major Prophets and Twelve Minor Prophets. They are called "major or minor prophets" because of the content of their writings and not because the writers were of legal age or power.
  - Major Prophets: Isaiah, Jeremiah, Lamentations, Ezekiel, and Daniel.
  - Minor Prophets: Hosea, Joel, Amos, Obadiah, Jonah, Micah, Nahum, Habakkuk, Zephaniah, Haggai, Zechariah, and Malachi.

The New Testament contains 27 Books; and are grouped as follows:

- Four biographical books: Matthew, Mark, Luke, and John.
- One historical book: Acts of the Apostles.
- Fourteen Pauline epistles: Romans, 1 and 2 Corinthians, Galatians, Ephesians, Philippians, Colossians, 1 and 2 Thessalonians, 1 and 2 Timothy, Titus, Philemon, and Hebrews.
- Seven pastoral epistles: James; 1 and 2 Peter; 1, 2 and 3 John; and Jude.
- One prophetic book: Apocalypse.

Sub-divisions of Chapters and Verses

In addition to the division in Old and New Testaments and in the different books; the Bible is organized into chapters and verses. This subdivision was carried out in the 13th century by Professor Esteban Langton of the University of Paris, as the books of the Bible were originally written in a single block. Thanks to this subdivision, any chapter or verse can be easily located, which facilitates its study and understanding.

- The Old Testament contains 929 chapters and 23,214 verses.
- The New Testament contains 260 Chapters and 7,959 verses.

How did the bible get to us?

When we study the Bible, we must ask ourselves, "How did this holy book come to us today?" We should consider that the Bible is not a common book, and it was not elaborated as we assume or are accustomed. The process for its elaboration was long and the Bible had to go through many phases to become what is today. In addition, we must consider that it was not printed as other books are today. The process included the minting of letters and symbols, printing on tables and stones and finally, the printing on paper. In this section we will detail a little about its origin and how it came to us.

Our Bible Comes from the Middle East

The Bible was written in an oriental language and environment. That is why it contains words, object names, cities, meals, and other artifacts used in those lands, but not ours. However, that does not mean that what is written does not apply to us. The Bible was written in the desert, in the city, in the countryside, and in many other places located in countries and cities in the Middle East.

Bible Languages

The Bible was written in languages other than our own. The Old Testament was written in Hebrew and some portions in Aramaic. The New Testament was written entirely in Greek. It is important to emphasize at this point that to understand the Bible, one must have notion of the differences of these languages and that the Bible that we have written in English had to go through a translation process. Today, we can receive help to better understand the original texts, thanks to the different dictionaries and aids that exist for a more accurate translation.

Materials

It should also be mentioned that the Bible went through a very specific process to which it would be recognized as "a book". It was initially written on different kinds of materials including stone, papyrus, parchment, skin; and, finally, printed into a paper book. In addition, the Bible was also written using different kinds of instruments, from chisels to ink pens. Today we enjoy being able to browse a well-crafted book, written in color and with images; but it was not always like this.

Inspiration of the Bible

The Bible is a sacred book, which contains the words and will of God, and its author is the Lord Almighty. However, we cannot rule out that it is also a human book, since it was written by men. As God is the author and not man, we must then understand that God used men to write His will and that they did not write what they wanted. Therefore, we must recognize that the word of God has come to us by divine inspiration and not by human will. That is, God inspired the biblical writers, and they wrote what God told them to write. Bancroft says it in a very precise way, "The writers were endowed with power and controlled in such a way by the Holy Spirit in the production of these writings, that they gave them divine and infallible authority."[9]

The following biblical verses confirm this truth:

> All scripture is given by inspiration of God, and is profitable for doctrine, for reproof, for correction, for instruction in righteousness: That the man of God may

---

[9] Emery H. Bancroft, Op. cit.,30.

be perfect, thoroughly furnished unto all good works. 2
Timothy 3:16–17

For the prophecy came not in old time by the will of
man: but holy men of God spoke as they were moved
by the Holy Ghost. 2 Peter 1:21

Why believe in the Bible?

If the Bible is the word of God, then we must believe in it. However,
many times we have heard people say, "Why should I believe in the
Bible, if it is a book that men wrote?" It is important to emphasize, as
we said earlier, that although it was written by men, God inspired it and
the men God used did not write what they wanted. Here are additional
reasons why we should believe in the Bible:

1. Because it is the Word of God.
   One must believe in it, for it is the word of God. The Bible
   is the record of God's relationships with men; therefore, we
   must believe all that is written. Every word written on its pages
   represents God's will for the human being.

2. Because it is the Safest Prophetic Word.
   The second reason why we should believe in the Bible is because
   everything in it is trustworthy. The same biblical text reads:

   We have also a more sure word of prophecy; whereunto
   ye do well that ye take heed, as unto a light that shineth
   in a dark place, until the day dawn, and the day star arise
   in your hearts. 2 Peter 1:19

This statement has to do with the truthfulness of God, for everything
He says has its strict fulfillment. Jesus said of this that neither a jack,
nor a period of the law would be without its compliance (Matthew 5:18).
Therefore, a child of God must know that the word is firm and secure,
and it should give him confidence and security.

3. For there is evidence of it being the word of God.
   In addition to the above, we must believe in the Bible because there is strong evidence that it is the word of God. At least two main points include:

First. Evidence in the Bible itself.

In many biblical texts, the Bible claims to be the Word of God. For example, in Exodus it says:

> "And the Lord said unto Moses, Write thou these words: for after the tenor of these words I have made a covenant with thee and with Israel." Exodus 34:27.

> In Jeremiah it says: "Thus speaketh the Lord God of Israel, saying, Write thee all the words that I have spoken unto thee in a book." Jeremiah 30:2.

> Texts like these declare repeatedly that what is written in the Bible is the word of God and that no one can contradict it.

Second. External evidence from the Bible.

Another guarantee to believe in the Bible is external evidence. Eternal evidence are those things that are said about the Bible or those considerations that determine its truthfulness. Here are four considerations presented by Larry S. Chafer:

a. The continuity of the Bible. The first external evidence of the Bible is continuity (Natural Union) with each other. One of the most surprising and extraordinary facts about the Holy Scriptures is that they were written by more than forty authors in a span of more than 1,600 years. However, the Bible is, "a book" and not a simple collection of 66 books. Its authors come from the most diverse places and situations of life. Among the authors are kings, peasants, philosophers, statesmen, fishermen, doctors, scholars, poets, and farmers. All lived in different cultures, in different existential experiences, and were often completely different in character. However, they all keep a unity in their writings. The Bible has a continuity that can be observed from Genesis to Revelation.

b. The extension of biblical revelation. In its manifestation of truth, the Bible is inextinguishable. Like a telescope, it explores the universe from the infinite heights and depths of the heavens to the tremendous depth of hell and captures God's works from beginning to end. As a microscope, it reveals the smallest details of God's plan and purpose and the most perfect work of creation.

c. The influence and publication of the Bible. No other book has ever been published in as many languages, by and for as many different peoples and cultures as the Bible itself. Its pages are among the first to be printed when the presses of the modern printing press were invented.

d. The Bible as literature. Considered literary work, the Bible is also supreme. It contains not only graphic history, but prophecy in detail, the most beautiful poetry and drama, stories of love and war, speculations of philosophy, and all that relates to biblical truth.[10]

Final Tips

Finally, we need to emphasize that as children of God, we must read the Bible periodically and learn it so that our lives will be changed by it. One of the first things I advise in my book, "La Vida Cristiana (The Christian life)" is to know why we should read it. In the same point that the Bible is God's voice and message for our lives, we can know God more intimately. Also, through it we can receive the teaching and instruction that our soul needs, and it correct us. Reading the Bible is necessary to live.[11]

---

[10] Lerry S. Chafer, *La Biblia: Palabra de Dios*, Seminario Reina Valera, http://www.seminarioabierto.com/doctrina101.htm., Retrieved April, 5, 2016.

[11] Roberto Tinoco, *La Vida Cristiana: Una guía bíblica para nuevos convertidos*, (Bloomington, IN: WestBow Press, 2016), 85-86.

Another recommendation for every believer is to establish a reading regime and be in constant contact with the Bible. Nowadays, there are many reading and devotional plans, which can help us approach and better understand the word of God. In the book, The Christian Life, it is noted that "the Bible must be read with a hungry heart to know the will of God, and with an open mind to be able to understand it". Since the Bible is as important to us, as children of God, then we must transmit it to our children and future generations, because it represents our most special treasure.[12]

Conclusion

We conclude this chapter by repeating that the Bible is the most important thing that we, as children of God, have. We must know the basic information of it, as well as the most outstanding details of it. What has been presented in this chapter, although simple, must be put it to work, because that will help us to know God better and His will for us.

---

[12] Ibid,89.

Chapter 3

God

≈

Hear, O Israel: The Lord our God is one Lord.

DEUTERONOMY 6:4

Knowing God is one of the greatest privileges that as human beings we can experience. God is the most wonderful being that exists, and just by studying about Him, our lives are blessed. Knowledge of God is the greatest thing a human being can achieve, but such knowledge is not easy to attain; for we are limited beings. However, God in His infinite mercy has made Himself known to us and allowed us to experience His presence. It is based on that kindness that we can talk about God and study God.

In this chapter we will learn some very important characteristics and attributes about God. For example: Who God is; about His existence and nature; and what is called and manifested to human beings – among other matters of paramount importance.

The Existence of God

As believers, the existence of God is the cornerstone of doctrine and our Christian life. There is no point in talking about God unless it is admitted that He exists and there is no point in gathering unless it is known that He is present. The Bible says of this:

> But without faith it is impossible to please him: for he that cometh to God must believe that he is, and that he is a rewarder of them that diligently seek him. Hebrews 11:6

Bancroft says it this way: "The existence of God is accepted as a fact in the scriptures without giving any argument to establish or prove it."[13]

Christians have no problem understanding and accepting that God exists; however, we must fight against various currents and thoughts of men who deny the existence of God.

Among those who deny are atheists who do not believe in God. There are also people who neither believe in nor claim that God exists. Sometimes these people demand Christians' response to their refusal of the Creator's existence. To prove the existence of God we have much to say, however, in this writing we will address only two things: first, the arguments in favor of the existence of God; and secondly, what the Bible says about God.

Rational Arguments in Favor of the Existence of God

In their book on Apologética (apologetics), Geiser and Brooks present four arguments for answering those who doubt or deny the existence of God, and are detailed below:

1. The cosmological argument. He argues that everything that exists in the world must have a proper cause. The famous "cause and effect" argument states that everything that exists must have been created. In other words, it exists for something and that "something" must be God. Paul said that all men know about God because God manifested Himself to them (Romans 1:19–20).

---

[13] Emery H. Bancroft, Op. cit., 42.

2. The teleological argument. It sustains the following: Anywhere the world looks at itself, it reveals intelligence, order, harmony, and design; thus, denouncing the existence of an intelligent being who designed this world.

3. The axiological argument or the moral law. This speaks of man's recognition of a higher good and his pursuit of moral ideal demands and needs the existence of a God who makes that ideal a reality.

4. The ontological argument. This argument holds that there must be an absolutely perfect being above all else and that human beings already have in their minds the idea of God.[14]

In addition to the four arguments presented above, Luis Berkhof adds one more, which is detailed below:

5. The historical or ethnological argument. Berkhof states: "Among the peoples and tribes of the earth is a feeling of the divine, which manifests itself in external worship." In other words, the individual feels the need for something transcendent in life, something that lifts him up and we see this reflected in the history of humanity. He also adds: "Being universal, this phenomenon must belong to the very nature of man."[15]

With the above mentioned, we can infer the following: It does not matter who man is, whatever his origin, or occupation; everyone usually experiences the feeling of a higher being. If we consider these arguments, we can see that man has received from God the intuition of His existence. We see this reflected in those who live in isolation from society, but have idols and worship them, thus teaching the need in mankind to worship something. Bancroft calls this "the argument of universal belief". This is precisely that in all parts of the world humans believe in a being or beings superior to whom they owe or have a responsibility.[16]

---

[14] N. Geiser y R. Brooks, *Apologética*, (Colombia, Editorial Unilit, revision 2003), 17-39.

[15] Louis Borkhof, *Teología Sistemática*, (Jenison, Michigan: T.E.L.L, 1988), 27-29.

[16] Emery H. Bancroft. Op. cit., 43-45.

Everything that we have presented above, is the work of God. God promotes His existence in the human being and is felt in such a way that even the most ignorant or the most intelligent person concludes that there is a "higher being". Someone whom we must worship or that somehow intervenes in human situations. We call this the natural affirmation of God's existence.

Biblical Proof of God's Existence

Not only do we acknowledge the existence of God by the world theologians and scholars, but the main proof of God's existence is the same word of God. The Bible offers a double revelation of God's existence.

First, it provides a revelation both in the nature around us, as well as in the human consciousness and providential government of this world. The other is embedded in each of the pages of our Bible. The first text of the Bible reads: In the beginning God created the heaven and the earth (Genesis 1:1). The first biblical verse does not begin to present God nor introduce Him as the intellectual author of the Bible. However, it is the recognition that God exists and that He does not need to prove anything concerning His existence. Not only does He exist, but He is also the creator of all things. Let's look at two classic examples of what we are referring to:

1. The heavens declare the glory of God; And the firmament sheweth his handiwork. Psalm 19:1 and Romans 1:19–20
2. God, who at sundry times and in diverse manners spoke in time past unto the fathers by the prophets, Hath in these last days spoken unto us by his Son, whom he hath appointed heir of all things, by whom also he made the worlds; Who being the brightness of his glory, and the express image of his person, and upholding all things by the word of his power, when he had by himself purged our sins, sat down on the right hand of the Majesty on high. Hebrews 1:1–3

The first passage reveals the existence of God through nature and the second reveals the existence of God through the Bible.

The Oneness of God

Now, believing in God is not a problem for those who are Christian nor for all those who, although not Christian, affirm the existence of God. Nevertheless, there is a question that many people ask themselves, "How many gods are there?" This question has long had the Christian world divided. Some say that God is one, others say no. Therefore, we must consider what the word of God teaches us about it.

When it comes to speaking and teaching about God, the Bible is clear about the answer it has for this question. James made it very clear as to whether God is one, two, or three. He wrote:

> Thou believest that there is one God; thou doest well: the devils also believe, and tremble. James 2:19

It is precisely these kinds of texts that establish what in the Christian world is known as "the oneness of God", but it also offers a concrete answer to what we are saying. Next, we will provide a broader picture of God's oneness.

Definition

The dictionary of the Royal Academy of the Spanish Language translates "oneness" as follows: (from the latin. Unicĭtas, -ātis). 1. F. Unique quality. The dictionary also states that this refers to the unity of God by asserting that God cannot be divided.[17] Interestingly, the dictionary emphasizes that "you can't divide." Therefore, when we refer to God, the word oneness speaks to us of quantity and the word unity,

---

[17] Diccionario de la lengua Española, Twentieth second edition, http://www.rae.es. Retrieved the 24 of July, 2019.

of integrity. Of God we could simply say that God is one and that one cannot be divided.

The message of God's oneness is as old as mankind. The historian, Josephus records that Abraham was the first to openly declare in the land of the Chaldeans that God is one. Because of this, the Chaldeans rose up against him and that was one of God's motivations for getting him out.[18]

The bible teaches that there is only one God.

When we study the Bible the subject Oneness, we discover that this doctrine is central to the biblical message. Both the Old and New Testaments clearly teach it. Despite the simplicity of this message and the clarity with which the Bible presents it, many who believe in God's existence have not understood it and continue to wonder whether God is one or more than one. Therefore, we consider it appropriate to mention some traditional texts to clarify this question.

The Old Testament teaches that there is only one God. The traditional expression of one God's doctrine is found in Deuteronomy 6:4 and says, "Hear, O Israel: The Lord our God is one Lord." This verse has become the most distinctive and important statement of faith for the Jews throughout the times. They call it "the shemá", which is the first word of the phrase in Hebrew, and they quote it frequently (at least three times a day). In the Old Testament, many verses of Scripture affirm that God is ONE.

The Ten Commandments begin with: "Thou shalt have no other gods before Me." (Exodus 20:3 and Deuteronomy 5:7). God emphasized this commandment when He declared that He is a jealous God (Exodus 20:5). Jealousy usually arises when there is a third party in a relationship. Therefore, God becomes jealous when we seek another god.

---

[18] Paul L Maier, *Josefo: Las Obras Esenciales*, (Grand Rapids, MI: Spokesperson, 1994) 24

In Deuteronomy 32:39, God said that there is no other god with Him. This means that there is no extra god to accompany our God. In addition, the scriptures say: Wherefore thou art great, O Lord God: for there is none like thee, neither is there any God beside thee, according to all that we have heard with our ears (2 Samuel 7:22; and 1 Chronicles 17:20). He alone is God (Psalm 86:10).

In the Old Testament, the prophet Isaiah is one of the greatest promoters of the Oneness because he makes several references stating there is only one God. Here are some:

- Before me there was no God formed, neither shall there be after me. Isaiah 43:10–11
- I am the first, and I am the last; and beside me there is no God. Isaiah 44:6
- Is there a God besides Me? yea, there is no God; I know not any. Isaiah 44:8
- I am the LORD that maketh all things; that stretcheth forth the heavens alone; that spreadeth abroad the earth by myself. Isaiah 44:24

Among many others...

The New Testament affirms that there is only one God. Jesus taught about Deuteronomy 6:4, calling it the first of all commandments (Mark 12:29–30). In addition, Jesus used verses like these many times.

We observe that the New Testament continues the teaching of the Old Testament of one God and explicitly repeats this message several times.

- Seeing it is one God, which shall justify. Romans 3:30
- There is none other God but one. I Corinthians 8:4
- But to us there is but one God, the Father. I Corinthians 8:6
- But God is one. Galatians 3:20
- One God and Father of all. Ephesians 4:6

- For there is one God. I Timothy 2:5
- Thou believest that there is one God; thou doest well: the devils also believe, and tremble. James 2:19

God is One and the whole Bible supports this thought. We must not accept the idea of a divided God or a pluralized divinity. God is and will be the only true God.

God

When we think of God, sometimes we ask ourselves, "What is God like? What does He look like physically? How tall is He?" We ask ourselves a lot of questions about God's divinity. Then we imagine God as a being like us, but we must know that God is very different from the human being. He is a very spiritual, transcendent, and an unimaginable being for our human mind, whom we often cannot understand. We will know God a little more closely and focus on two specific areas: namely His nature and attributes.

The Nature of God

The nature of an individual refers to the unique properties of a being or individual, in this case of God. In addition, it also refers to the composures and the forms that are constituted internally and externally. When we refer to God, we have learned that, since the beginning of time, humans have tried and sought a way to project or present God through literary images, figures, paintings, and descriptions, but have always fallen short.

Bancroft tells us that the nature of God is best revealed by his attributes, and that the attributes of God are those essential, permanent, and distinctive characteristics that can be affirmed regarding His being.[19]

---

[19] Emery H. Bancroft. Op. cit. 47-48.

God is Spirit

Perhaps one of the most powerful statements regarding God's nature is given to us by our Lord Jesus Christ. Jesus affirms that God is a Spirit (John 4:24) and that a Spirit has no flesh or bones (Luke 24:39). Based on this affirmation of Christ, we must rethink our minds to establish that God neither looks nor is anything like a human being.

God is Spirit – from Gr. Pneo: Air, breath (blast). This changes everything in our conception of God because He doesn't have any bones and does not have a body as we have. Although the Bible says that God made man in his image (Genesis 1:27), we must clarify that this image is not necessarily physical.

It is important to explain that in the previous paragraph we are not talking about the humanity of Christ, a matter that we will address later, but that we refer to the essence of what God is really like a being, that is, His individual characteristics only. Since God is spirit, He forbids us to make an image of Him, or to compare Him to anything. In Deuteronomy 4:15–20 God forbids the worship of any being or thing created outside of God and for human beings to compare God to any creature in this world or spiritual world. In verse 15, He clearly says, "Take careful heed to yourselves, for you saw no form when the LORD spoke to you at Horeb out of the midst of the fire."

Worshipping any object, image, or likeness of something divine outside of God is regarded in the Bible as idolatry. Many people in their attempt to know what God's physiognomy is seek here and there, but nothing that human beings seek will be able to satisfy that quest since no one has ever seen God. At least those were John's words. No man hath seen God at any time, the only begotten Son, which is in the bosom of the Father, he hath declared him (John 1:18). Obviously, this statement refers precisely to what we have been saying about the nature of God.

The Attributes of God

The second point we must consider regarding God has to do with His attributes. Theologists recognize that one of the best ways to know God is through His attributes. Attributes are defined as each of the qualities or properties of a being.[20] When we study God, we discover that He has many attributes that belong only to Him and that we as human beings cannot attain, but there are certain attributes which He has shared us.

God is Omnipotent

God's first attribute is omnipotence. The word omnipotent means "all powerful". This means that God has no limitation and is not subject to any human law. Furthermore, it means that He can do everything. We are subject to the law of gravity, but God is not; we are subject to the law of speed, but God is not. God does not get tired, fatigued, He doesn't sleep, or needs to walk because He can move back and forth without problems. God can do everything (Genesis 35:11). Sometimes we do not understand what the omnipotence of God means because our minds are very limited. Suffice it to say, God can draw water from the stones (Numbers 20:8) or make them speak (Luke 19:40); and open the sea (Exodus 14:16–22) or the sky (Luke 3:21). Nevertheless, anything imaginable and unimaginable, God can do it.

God is Omnipresent

God is also omnipresent. The word omnipresent means that "God is present everywhere". He is present everywhere at the same time because God is spirit. God is the only spirit that is truly omnipresent; for all other spiritual beings such as demons, angels, and Satan himself can be confined to a certain space (Mark 5:10; Jude 1:6; Revelation 20:1–3), but God does not.

---

[20] *Real Academia Española*, http://lema.rae.es/drae/?val=Atributo. Retrieved 24 July 2019.

Sometimes we cannot understand how God makes himself to be everywhere at the same time, but that is one of the characteristics of our God. Otherwise, He would not be God. God's omnipresence means that when a group of people gather in the city of Miami, and at the same time, a group of brothers gather in Los Angeles, God can be in both places. Thus, both groups experience the wonderful presence of the Lord.

God is Omniscient

God's third attribute is omniscience. The word means that God knows everything. Psalm 139:1–6 teaches us that God knows everything, including our movements, thoughts, habits, ways, and words. Job confessed:

> I know that thou canst do everything, and that no thought can be withholden from thee. Job 42:2.

God has complete knowledge of everything, including knowledge of the future (Acts 2:23). It is wonderful to know that there is nothing hidden before God that He does not know. The Psalmist said:

> For there is not a word in my tongue, but, lo, O Lord, thou knowest it altogether. Psalm 134:4.

The Lord not only knows the words we are going to speak, but also what will happen in the future with us.

God is Immense

When we think of God, we must imagine that God is very great, not only in works and power, but in dimension. God fills everything; He is great, and His presence covers the whole earth. God Himself said:

The heaven is my throne, and the earth is my footstool: where is the house that ye build unto me? and where is the place of my rest? (Isaiah 66:1).

Although no one has ever seen God as He is (John 1:18), and although some biblical passages can be interpreted as symbolic, in many biblical verses God speaks of Himself as someone who is very large in size. For example, in Isaiah, God asks:

Who hath measured the waters in the hollow of his hand, and meted out heaven with the span, and comprehended the dust of the earth in a measure, and weighed the mountains in scales, and the hills in a balance? Isaiah 40:12.

Although this text can also be interpreted as symbolic, the greatness of God is immeasurable. God is so great, that He can measure the water in the hollow of his hand. God is great!

God is Holy

Perhaps one of the most significant things we should consider about God's attributes is His holiness. He is extremely holy. He dwells in holiness and purity and in Him sin is never found, let alone some thought of wickedness. His ways are paths of righteousness. His works are never ill-intentioned, for he does not inhabit any bad thing. That is why He commanded his people to be sanctified and live a holy life (Leviticus 20:7).

God is Just

One of God's most favorable characteristics for human beings is His righteousness. God is just in all His ways and will always fight for the righteous, just, and true (Deuteronomy 32:4). He who believes in God is confident that God judges all things according to His equity and mercy. Perhaps this is one of God's most wonderful attributes in relation to human beings. It does not matter if men do not do us justice, God always will.

Obviously, this also has its consequences, because for this to be done, we must act in accordance with God's righteousness.

God is Love

Another of God's most experienced attributes by human beings, especially by Christians, is love. The Bible says that God is love (1 John 4:8). We have heard this phrase many times in our churches and have surely embraced it, especially when we have been rejected or treated badly. God has loved us in such a special way that He gave His only begotten son to die for us on the cross of Calvary (John 3:16).

Other Characteristics of God

Other characteristics or attributes that God possesses are individuality, personality, and rationality. That is, God is an intelligent being with a will (Romans 9:19) and can reason (Isaiah 1:18). He possesses an intelligent mind (Romans 11:33–34). The fact that man is an emotional being indicates that God has emotions, for God created man in his image (Genesis 1:27).

Conclusion

As we have seen in this chapter, knowing God is an extraordinary occurrence that can happen to human beings. Through what has been presented we can have a broader idea about the God we serve and are able to approach Him in a different way than we may be accustomed to. Therefore, I hope that this chapter will help us know and fall in love with that great and loving God.

Chapter 4

The Manifestations of God

≈

And without controversy great is the mystery of godliness: God was manifest in the flesh, justified in the Spirit, seen of angels, preached unto the Gentiles, believed on in the world, received up into glory.

1 TIMOTHY 3:16

In the chapter before, we mention that God is spirit and that a spirit has no flesh or bones. So, if God is spirit, how can we know Him? Furthermore, how can we touch Him or see Him? It is precisely in this area that we need to know about God's manifestations. God has revealed Himself to mankind through time and by different means. These kinds of revelations are called "The Manifestations of God." In this chapter we will address the different ways by which God has made himself known to human beings.

Definition

According to the Vine dictionary, the word "manifestation" comes from Greek anadeixis, which means "publicly display" and from fanerosis, (faneroo) which means "make visible, clear, manifest, known". We define that a manifestation of God is a method God uses to make himself known or to show Himself to human beings. It is important to mention, that if it were not for these revelations, the human being would never have known anything of God. There are several manifestations or ways of showing God to human beings and we will consider them below.[21]

Theophanies

One of the ways God revealed Himself in the Old Testament and dealt with man was using theophanies, (from the Gr. epiphaneia, appearance). In fact, theophanies are the most important manifestations we have in the Old Testament. Because of these theophanies, we can know much about our great God and Savior.

Bishop David K. Bernard, a Pentecostal professor, speaks to us about theophanies and states: "A theophany is a visible manifestation of God, and we usually regard it as temporary."[22] Being that God is invisible to man, for He is spirit, He must manifest Himself in some physical form to become visible. This makes it possible for the human being to be able to look at Him, hear Him, and even touch Him.

God's manifestations have been very common over time as God has always wanted to be in touch with His creation. In biblical history there were several men of God who had the privilege of seeing God in a clear way, who was manifested to them in different ways.

Abraham

Patriarch Abraham had many encounters and visions with God. Through the scriptures we realize that God appeared to him in a vision and spoke to him concerning the plans He had for him. The Lord also descended visibly, when Abraham prepared an altar and split the animals in half as a sacrifice. God presented himself in a smoking oven and as a torch of fire and passed through the divided animals (Genesis 15). He also appeared to Abraham as a man and two angels

---

[21] *Enciclopedia Electrónica Ilumina,* Vine Diccionario Expositivo, (Orlando FL Caribe- Betania, 2005).
[22] David K. Bernard, *La unicidad de Dios,* Teología Pentecostal, Vol. 1, 1993.

who accompanied him while he was in the plains of Mambre and spoke to him and ate a prepared meal (Genesis 18). As we can see in this example, God first used fire to show Himself to Abraham, but then appeared to him in the form of a human being.

Jacob

Another character who had the great privilege of seeing God face to face was Jacob. God appeared to Jacob in a dream and told him about the promises made to Abraham and how those promises would be kept in him. In addition, on another occasion He appeared as a man, as He had to Abraham (Genesis 28:12–16; 32:24–32). In Genesis 32, Jacob fought with the man and proclaimed, "For I have seen God face-to-face …". The Bible also describes this appearance of God as "the angel" (Hosea 12:4). GOD manifested Himself to Jacob as face-to-face and used this opportunity to fight with him and to bless him. We must clarify that if Jacob fought with the angel (God) for a blessing, it is because God obviously let Himself be touched by Jacob and not because God is weak.

Moses

A third example was the great legislator, Moses. He had a lot of experiences with God in which God presented Himself in various forms. On the first occasion, God appeared to Moses as a burning bush which was not consumed. From there, God called him to deliver His people from Egypt. In another words, God was in the flame of fire and spoke to Moses. He also appeared to him in a cloud of glory and fire on Mount Sinai; spoke to him face-to-face in the Tabernacle; and on another occasion showed him His back, but not His face (Exodus 3:1–10; 24:12–18; 33:9–11; 33:18–23). Moses had great experiences with God, but without a doubt, the most impressive of all was when he was on the mountain for forty days and forty nights. When Moses descended his face was radiant to such an extent that he had to cover his face with a veil so that he could speak to the people (Exodus 34:27–35).

Several of the prophets had visions of God.

Other great men of God had experiences with the Most High, but because of space we will not mention them all; although, we will mention some briefly. Isaiah saw God on His throne, heard His voice, and was entrusted by God with a job (Isaiah 6). God showed Ezekiel a vision concerning His glory. In the vision Ezekiel sees the living beings around the throne and on the throne, one sitting in the likeness of a man (Ezekiel 1).

God also appeared to Ezekiel in the form of a man, engulfed in fire, (Ezekiel 8:1–4). God manifested Himself to Daniel in a night vision as the Ancient of Days (Daniel 7:2–9). When Daniel's friends were cast in the fiery furnace, they were visited by fourth man, who according to Nebuchadnezzar, was like a god (Daniel 3). Many others looked at God on different occasions and in different ways, teaching us of God's great desire to communicate with mankind and demonstrate His interest in us.

The Triple Manifestation of God

Although God has manifested Himself to human beings in many ways, as previously mentioned, one of the most important is the triple manifestation of God. However, this form of revelation is one of the most difficult for many Christians to understand as they often confuse God's interaction regarding the Father, the Son, and the Holy Spirit. The problem is to assume that God is three different persons and one true God. This statement goes against the word of God because the Bible teaches that God is ONE (Deuteronomy 6:4). We must also clarify that, although God is a personal God, the word "person" is not applicable to God, for God is Spirit.

The church of Jesus Christ traditionally believes that God is One both numerically and integrally, so it is understood that God has manifested himself in three different ways:

- As a Father in creation,
- As Son in redemption, and
- As the Holy Spirit in the lives of believers.

Although this will be explained later, it is worth saying that they are not three different people and much less three different gods, but the same God who has manifested Himself in three different ways. Based on this statement and understanding it, it will be much easier to explain several texts in which the three manifestations appear interacting with each other. One of the most revealing texts of the New Testament is found in Paul's letter to Timothy when he says:

> And without controversy great is the mystery of godliness: God was manifest in the flesh, justified in the Spirit, seen of angels, preached unto the Gentiles, believed on in the world, received up into glory. 1 Timothy 3:16

Paul says that God manifested Himself in the flesh in the person of Jesus Christ; because that was the only way He could come into this world and rescue it. Later, we will study what this consists of, but suffice it to say for now that God has manifested Himself as Father in creation, as Son in redemption, and as the Holy Spirit in the consolation of believers.

The Name of God

Another of the theological confusions in Christianity has to do with the name of God. The question is simple, what is the name of God? This question can be answered in many ways; however, it depends on who is asked. For some, the name of God may be Jehovah and for others it is Jesus Christ. However, in the Bible, God says he has a name, but it was not known to Abraham, Isaac, and Jacob (Exodus 6.2-3). God not only revealed Himself in many ways, but also revealed his name, and that is what we are interested in knowing.

The Importance of Names in the Bible

Before we go any further, we should talk about the importance of names in the Bible. The use of names in biblical times, especially in the Old Testament, had greater meaning than they have today. According to David Bernard, people often used names to reveal some of the individual's character, history, or nature. For example, Abraham means fathers of multitudes; Jacob means impersonator; Peter means stone; etc. Similarly, when we study the name or names God has used for Himself, they too have a special meaning.[23]

The Revelation of God's Name

God has used different methods to reveal himself to mankind. In one of these methods, He used different names or titles with which He identifies Himself. To know the name of God is to know Him. This is how the name of God represented His presence, the revelation of His character, and the revelation of His power. In addition to the above we can observe three important points as we study the name of God.

The name of God is one of the links in identifying Jesus with God. We could connect Him with Jesus Christ through the names that God used. One name is Emmanuel (Matthew 1:23) which was given to Jesus, meaning "God with us".

The name of God has always been an enigma for many people, and this is another point to consider. Since the beginning of time, the name of God has been hidden from mankind, and we ask ourselves, "Why?"

Inquiring about the name of God was something that the ancients had from very early on in the Bible.

---

[23] David K. Bernard, *La Unicidad de Dios*, Teología Pentecostal, Vol. 1, 1993.

The Mystery of God's Name

In the Bible we find individuals who inquired about and even asked God for His name, yet God did not give them the answer or at least did not have a clear answer to their question. Let's look at some examples:

1. Jacob asked God for His name as he was fighting for his blessing in Peniel. The text says, "And Jacob asked him, and said, Tell me, I pray thee, thy name …" (Genesis 32:29).

However, God did not tell him, but on the contrary, he asks, "why do you ask me by name?"

2. Moses also asks God for His name when he is called to take Israel out of Egypt. Moses says to God:

"And Moses said unto God, Behold, when I come unto the children of Israel, and shall say unto them, The God of your fathers hath sent me unto you; and they shall say to me, What is his name? What shall I say unto them?" (Exodus 3:13).

This was a direct question to God, and it was very important because God was sending him as His representative to Egypt with a task of freeing Israel from slavery. Moses thought it was normal to know who was sending him. What was God's response to Moses? Exodus 3:14 contains God's answer to Moses's question, "And God said unto Moses, I Am That I Am: and he said, Thus shalt thou say unto the children of Israel, I Am hath sent me unto you." Exodus 3:14

If we pay close attention to this, we can see that the discussion has to do with the name of the one who is sending Moses. This is the clearest opportunity God has to reveal his name and yet God does not say, "My name is such," but rather He says, "I Am who I Am". In other words, God does not answer the question. Later, when Moses is already in Egypt talking to the people of Israel, the Bible relates this:

"And God spake unto Moses, and said unto him, I am the Lord: And I appeared unto Abraham, unto Isaac, and unto Jacob, by the name of God Almighty, but by my name Jehovah was I not known to them." Exodus 6:2–3.

In this text we can see that God uses the phrase "I am Jehovah" and "by my name Lord did not make myself known to them" and we must ask ourselves, what is God really saying with these words? The name of Jehovah is mentioned for the first time here from God, (although we will address this point later) yet it seems that this is not enough, because he still wonders for the name of God as we will see later.

3. Manoa also asks for the name of God when God appears to him to give him the good news that his wife will have a child, who will be Samson. "And Manoah said unto the angel of the Lord, What is thy name, that when thy sayings come to pass we may do thee honour?" Judges 13:17. Manoa dared and asked God, but God only answers the following, "And the angel of the Lord said unto him, Why askest thou thus after my name, seeing it is secret?" Judges 13:18

Thus, this man also did not get an answer from the Lord concerning the name of God.

4. After reviewing the above, we have a revealing question from the prophet Agur. "What is his name, and what is his son's name, if thou canst tell?" Proverbs 30:4

This prophet asks for the name of God and even adds, the name of his son. However, there is no answer for him either.

5. God's answer. Recognizing that His people are asking for His name God says through the prophet Isaiah:

"Therefore my people shall know my name: therefore, they shall know in that day that I am he that doth speak: behold, it is I." Isaiah 52:6

This text is very revealing because it teaches that God Himself will come to earth to reveal His name. When Jesus came to earth, he said that he had come precisely to reveal the name of the Father.

> And I have declared unto them thy name, and will declare it: that the love wherewith thou hast loved me may be in them, and I in them. John 17:26.

But, the question at the beginning of this chapter still stands, What is the name of God?

The Names and Titles of God in the Bible

Before we go any further, we should talk a little bit about the names that God has given himself throughout biblical history and from there we will depart with our conclusions.

When we review biblical history, we can find that God has self-appointed himself with some names and titles that reflect his character and personality. On the other hand, it is worth mentioning that the revelation of his name has been progressive and not immediate, that is; God gradually manifested His name. Among the most used in writing we have the following:

1. Elohim. (Genesis 1:1) This name appears as early as the beginning of things. It is commonly translated as "gods"; but its meaning is plurality of majesty or virtues and not necessarily many gods.
2. El-Elyon. It means the tallest or the highest (Genesis 14:18).
3. Adonai. It means LORD. (Genesis 15:2–8). This has been used a multitude of times in the scriptures.
4. El-Shaday. It means the Almighty God (Genesis 17:1).
5. El-Olam. It means Eternal God or Eternal (Genesis 21:33).
6. Jehovah. It means "He that exists by himself." This is the most used name in the Old Testament, and the name the Jews

adopted as the official name of God. The word comes from the Hebrew text: YHVH and is found in Exodus 3:14.

It is important that we mention that from this Bible passage arises the famous Tetragramton: (YHVH). To which the vowels of the name Adonai were added, (YaHoVaH) to read it, because the Hebrew vocabulary lacks vowels. A group of religious called the Masoretes invented a vocal system back in the ninth century AD which allowed us to read it better. That's where the name of Jehovah came from.

All these names were used to refer to God however none of them is a proper name, since they are all significant or wanted to say something. It was not until Christ came to earth that he brought true revelation of God's name as we will look at the next chapter.

Conclusion

We conclude by emphasizing that God in His great mercy has manifested Himself to human beings in many ways and forms, with the manifestation in the flesh being the greatest of all. It is through these manifestations that we can know Him and experience His love and mercy; but it is also because of them that we can understand many of the mysteries that have been hidden since the creation of the world, especially those that relate to Jesus Christ. In addition, we can learn how God relates to human beings and how we can understand a little bit about His way of being and acting.

Chapter 5

Jesus Christ

≋

When Jesus came into the coasts of Caesarea Philippi, he asked his disciples, saying, Whom do men say that I the Son of man am?

MATTHEW 16:13

For Christians, the topic of Jesus Christ is one of the most exciting subjects and it is one of the most discussed, treated, and written about by most of our pastors and writers. However, it is important to emphasize that this chapter does not provide every aspect pertaining to Christology, rather it provides a brief description of what Jesus Christ means to all of us who have decided to follow Him. In this chapter we will address issues related to the identity of Jesus Christ and discuss His nature and deity. We will also provide insight to His humanity and His relationship with divinity.

Who is Jesus?

We must begin this chapter by focusing on the most important question of all time, which has kept many Christians in check: "Who is Jesus?" Since the time of Jesus, people have inquired over this. Even Jesus himself asked His disciples in Matthew 16:13: "Whom do men say that I the Son of man am?" This verse highlights the fact that Jesus was interested in knowing what His disciples thought of Him. This question, which is still being asked today, has to do with the identity of Jesus Christ. Dr. Fortino in a Christology exhibition mentions that the problems that exist in Christianity today, are in direct correlation with the identity of Jesus Christ.[24]

For many, Jesus was a prophet or a teacher. At least, that is what the disciples said in Matthew 16:14 when they answered Jesus saying, "Some say that thou art John the Baptist: some, Elijah; and others, Jeremiah, or one of the prophets." Now for us, who is Jesus? Interestingly, many people are still asking themselves this today because they still do not know who Jesus is. To answer this question, we must consider some biblical texts in which Jesus Christ is presented in different manifestations.

Jesus is the Messiah or Christ, the Son of God

One of Jesus's first statements about His person and identity is found in the Apostle Peter's reply to Jesus's question. Jesus asks His disciples, "Who do you say I am?" and Peter answers saying, "Thou art the Christ, the Son of the living God. And Jesus answered and said unto him, Blessed art thou, Simon Bar-Jona: for flesh and blood hath not revealed it unto thee, but my Father which is in heaven." (Matthew 16:16–17)

Here begins God's first revelation about Christ. According to this verse, Jesus is the Christ, the son of the living God. Now, "the Christ" in Greek or "Messiah" in Hebrew – which both translate to "the anointed" – was precisely who the Jews were waiting for. We see this well marked in Jesus's encounter with the first disciples. Let us look at some incidents in which a revelation is given concerning the identity of Christ as the Messiah.

The first incident we see is when Andrew testifies to Peter concerning Jesus and says, "We have found the Messiah, which is, being interpreted, the Christ" (John 1:41). This passage clearly shows not only what we are saying, but it also demonstrates the translation from Hebrew to

---

[24] J. Fortino, *Cristología*, Florida Bible College (Miami, FL June 13, 2009) 3-4.

Greek. Messiah, or Christ, is the same title given to Jesus by these first disciples. Jesus is the anointed of God who was to come into this world.

In John 1:43–49 another incident occurs when Jesus finds Philip and asks him to follow Him. Philip then finds Nathanael and tells him almost the same words mentioned by Andrew to Peter: "We have found him, of whom Moses in the law, and the prophets, did write, Jesus of Nazareth, the son of Joseph" (John 1:45). Let us note here the revelation of his words: they had found the one whom Moses and the prophets had written about and they identified him as Jesus the son of Joseph the carpenter.

Another incident takes place in the same chapter, verses 47–49. Philip brings Nathanael before Jesus and the Master flatters him for being a true Israelite in which there is no deception. Nathaniel, surprised, then asks Jesus where he knows him from. Jesus reveals to Nathanael that before Philip called him, Jesus had already seen him under a fig tree. This word was very strong for Nathanael, because even though Jesus was not present when Philip called him, He knew he was under the fig tree. This incident culminates with the following exclamation by Nathanael: "Rabbi, thou art the Son of God; thou art the King of Israel" (John 1:49). Let us note here that this true Israelite in whom there is no deception exclaims two words with prophetic inclusion: "You are the Son of God" and "You are the King of Israel". These two terms will be discussed later but suffice it now to say that the Messiah-Christ is precisely the King of Israel.

Finally, the Bible records another meaningful event in another passage: Jesus's conversation with the Samaritan woman (John 4:5–42). Jesus asked her for water to drink and shared words with her regarding true worship, which, according to Jesus, is given in spirit and in truth. This conversation causes her to express what the Israelites knew very well, concerning the coming of the Messiah into this world. The woman saith unto him, "I know that the Messias cometh, which is called Christ: when he is come, he will tell us all things" (John 4:25). We can appreciate two important things in this statement:

1. They were waiting for the Messiah or Christ to come and
2. He would have all the answers.

Jesus saith unto her, "I that speak unto thee am He" (John 4:26). Here, Jesus openly declares himself as the Christ or the anointed one of God who was to come into the world. The anointed one of God, was the manifestation of God in the flesh, by which God would deliver His people from sin.

Jesus is the Incarnated God

Another point to consider is that Jesus is the incarnated God; that is, the God who becomes human. We must emphasize that the base of God's manifestations is God's desire to make Himself known to human beings. God is spirit, and the only way God established for us to know Him is through manifestations, one being in the flesh.

To explain this important point, let's look at two different passages from the prophet Isaiah that have a direct relationship with Jesus Christ and tell us about the incarnation. In the first text, God says through the prophet: "Therefore the Lord himself shall give you a sign; Behold, a virgin shall conceive, and bear a son, and shall call his name Immanuel." (Isaiah 7:14). This verse speaks of the sign that God is giving to the house of David, and it indicates that a virgin will conceive (something impossible for humans) and give birth to a child. In addition, it clarifies that the child who will be born will be called "Immanuel" which means "God with us" (according to Matthew 1:23).

We can see that there is a clear reference to Jesus Christ in this passage for two reasons:

1. Mary has been the only virgin that has conceived without having been with a man in the entire history of mankind. (To read all about this miracle, see Luke 1:26–38).
2. This refers to the divinity of Jesus, which we will see later.

A second message revealed in Isaiah which also has a direct relationship with Jesus is found in chapter nine verse six:

"For unto us a child is born, unto us a son is given: and the government shall be upon his shoulder: and his name shall be called Wonderful, Counsellor, The mighty God, The everlasting Father, The Prince of Peace." Isaiah 9:6

This passage clearly shows the theological implications of prophecy. The child to be born will have a very powerful divine burden and will have upon his shoulder the complete deity. He will be called: "the Admirable" who did not want to give his name to Manoa (Judges 13:18), "the Counselor", "the Strong God", "the Eternal Father", and the "Prince of Peace"; all divine implications. These two passages given by the prophet Isaiah shed light to understand the character of the child who would be born would be the Messiah expected by Israel.

The other matter to consider regarding the incarnated God, concerns the fulfillment of the prophecies mentioned by Isaiah. We can find the fulfilment of this prophesy in the gospel of Matthew, when the angel of the Lord appears to Joseph to persuade him not to leave Mary, his fiancée, because what is in her womb is the work of the Holy Spirit. The angel gives precise details concerning not only the fulfillment of the prophecy but also the identity and name of the Messiah.

"And she shall bring forth a son, and thou shalt call his name Jesus: for he shall save his people from their sins. Now all this was done, that it might be fulfilled which was spoken of the Lord by the prophet, saying, Behold, a virgin shall be with child, and shall bring forth a son, and they shall call his name Immanuel, which being interpreted is, God with us." Matthew 1:21–23.

We can see that what Isaiah had prophesied had now had its fulfillment and was confirmed by the angel of the Lord, leaving no doubt that what the prophet had said was regarding Jesus. This child is the Messiah, and the name Immanuel was replaced by Jesus in a clear allusion that He was truly the God who would become flesh.

In another passage parallel to this, but given by Luke, the same line of thought is observed concerning the details of the identity and role of the child who was born.

"For unto you is born this day in the city of David a Savior, which is Christ the Lord." Luke 2:11

Jesus is presented by the angel as a savior, who is also the Christ. Therefore, we can conclude that our Lord Jesus Christ was the Messiah awaited by Israel and the incarnated God who was to come into this world to save sinners. Since God cannot die because He is God, He became human in Jesus so that He could perform the miracle of salvation through His death on the cross of Calvary.

The Nature of Jesus Christ

One of the dilemmas concerning Jesus' identity is about His nature. Is Jesus God? Is He human? Or what does He constitute? These have been the most difficult questions to answer and have created many divisions among Christians. To better understand this matter, we must consider some things that speak to us concerning the nature of Jesus Christ.

Revelation must be received from God.

The first thing a Christian must recognize is that it takes revelation from God to understand the nature of God. In this case, this revelation must be interpreted as that light of understanding to comprehend what the Scriptures are telling us. For example, let us see the words of Jesus: concerning what we are saying: "In that hour Jesus rejoiced in spirit, and said, I thank thee, O Father, Lord of heaven and earth, that thou hast hid these things from the wise and prudent, and hast revealed them unto babes: even so, Father; for so it seemed good in thy sight. All things are delivered to me of my Father: and no man knoweth who the Son is, but the Father; and who the Father is, but the Son, and he to whom the Son will reveal him." (Luke 10:21–22).

In this Biblical passage our Lord clearly hints that a person can be very wise and intelligent, however, if God does not reveal His mysteries to him, he will not be able to understand them. It is strange, but in order to know and understand who Jesus is, divine revelation is necessary.

Many times, we struggle for someone to understand this, but what is needed is God's divine revelation for that person. Peter received this on that occasion when Christ asked his disciples about who he was and Peter answered him saying, "And Simon Peter answered and said, Thou art the Christ, the Son of the living God." (Matthew 16:16). The Apostle answered this question without hesitation, while the other peers gave other answers. For this reason, Jesus said to him, "Blessed art thou, Simon Bar-Jona: for flesh and blood hath not revealed it unto thee, but my Father which is in heaven." (Matthew 16:17). Therefore, it takes God's revelation to understand who Jesus is. It doesn't matter how much knowledge a person can have, without the revelation of God, a person will never be able to understand this great truth of the word of God.

To support this way of thinking we must observe the rest of the Lord's disciples, but more specifically Philip and Thomas. In John 14, we see them both uncertain towards the identity of Jesus. In verse 5, Thomas appears not to know where Jesus is going, let alone knows the way. In verse 8, Philip asks Jesus to show them the "Father." Jesus confronts him for not knowing him after walking together for so long (John 14:9–10). Thus, we can further comprehend that if these men who walked closely with Jesus, did not know Him, how much less a person could know Jesus two thousand plus years later. That is why God's divine revelation is necessary to know Jesus.

Understanding the Dual Nature of Jesus

The second thing to consider when seeking the answer to who Jesus is has to do with the "double nature of Jesus". In Jesus there were two natures: a human nature and a divine nature. When we talk about two natures, we mean that Jesus was a human being, to the full extent of the word, but He was also divine. This matter of the dual nature of Jesus will be explain later. Suffice it now to understand that our Lord Jesus Christ was a man, but he was also God. The prophet Isaiah prophesied of this when he said, "and his name shall be called Wonderful, Counsellor, the mighty God, the everlasting Father, the Prince of Peace" (Isaiah 9:6). Jesus is then the God who became man and in whom dwelled the whole fulness of the deity (Colossians 2:9).

Now, it is important to emphasize that when we understand the dual nature of Jesus, it will be easy to understand other biblical texts in which Jesus interacts with the Father or the Holy Spirit. However, when this key point is not understood, it becomes difficult to comprehend other biblical texts and that is where misinterpretations arise.

Jesus Christ is God

The Bible fervently teaches that Jesus Christ is God. But if this is a truth of the word of God, how do we explain Jesus's relationship with God? And, where did we leave the "Jehovah" of the Old Testament? The Bible clearly declares that Jehovah is God (Deuteronomy 6:4). This is where these questions arise: "Are there two gods? Or is it the same God?" In this next segment we will try to explain it in the simplest way possible. To explain Jesus's Divinity, it is necessary that we consider some indispensable truths about Jesus's relationship with God.

The Father-Son Dilemma

One of the great dilemmas in understanding the divinity of Jesus, is the Father-Son relationship of Jesus with God. Let us understand that we mention the "Father" we are referring to God. One of the examples of this relationship is that Jesus spoke a lot about His Father. "My Father, which gave them me, is greater than all; and no man can pluck them out of my Father's hand. I and My Father are one" (John 10:29–30).

This dilemma is resolved when we apply the dual nature of Jesus Christ in the interpretation of this text. Jesus as a man or Son needed to have his

Father; for God is the Father of all creation and even of Christ. However, in his divinity, Jesus was God and, therefore, on many occasions He made decisions for Himself.

What about when Jesus prays? Who does He pray to?

Many have an issue understanding passages where Jesus prayed to the Father, and they say that Jesus is another person. For example, let us consider the following biblical text: "These words spake Jesus, and lifted up his eyes to heaven, and said, Father, the hour is come; glorify thy Son, that thy Son also may glorify thee" (John 17:1). In this passage, we must understand that Jesus as a man needed to direct his prayer to the Father, for prayers must be addressed to Him. This is where Jesus's double nature must be applied. This passage can then be interpreted as follows: The humanity of God (Christ) prays to His own Divinity (God).

Jesus as man and as God.

The other issue is the dynamic that exists in the dual nature of Jesus as a man, but also as God. To better understand Jesus's relationship with God, we must consider several events in which Jesus acts as God and as a man interchangeably. Let's look at the following table:

Table 1	
Jesus, as a man:	Jesus, as God:
He was hungry. Mat. 4:2	He fed crowds. Mat. 15:32–39
He had to sleep. Mat. 8:24	He did not need to sleep. Rev. 1:8
He had to pray. Mat. 26:39	He answered prayers. Jn. 14:13
He was tired. Jn. 4:6	He doesn't get tired. Rev. 1:8
He had to learn. Heb. 5:8	He knew everything. Jn 2:25

In the table above, Jesus as a man, is hungry, but as God, He feeds multitudes. Jesus as a man, must pray, but as God, He answers prayers. Jesus as a man, had to learn, but as God, He knows everything. In this table, the two natures that Jesus possessed are clearly seen and we can broadly understand all those texts that sometimes show Jesus addressing the Father and vice versa.

The New Testament Affirms that Jesus is God

In the Bible we can find several biblical texts in which it is affirmed that Jesus is God. These passages are also very clear. Let's see some.

In Romans - Paul tells the Romans this: "Whose are the fathers, and of whom as concerning the flesh Christ came, who is over all, God blessed forever. Amen." (Romans 9:5). Note that this verse deals with two very important points:

1. Christ came "according to the flesh". This means that God came in the flesh, and therefore, Jesus has all the characteristics of a human being.
2. Paul calls Christ "God above all things". This is a title that the Lord claims only for Himself: "Thus saith the Lord the King of Israel, and his redeemer the Lord of hosts; I am the first, and I am the last; and beside me there is no God" (Isaiah 44:6).

Romans 9:5 presents a very serious predicament for those who insist on separating Jesus Christ from God. The issue is that Paul presents Jesus as "God above all things," thus calling into question Isaiah's words about the Lord. Therefore, we must ask ourselves the following questions: "Is Jesus a different God to Jehovah?"; "Are they two different gods?"; "Or is Jesus the same Jehovah himself?" The answer to this is resolved if we recognize that the entire Bible establishes that there is only one God. To say that there is more than one God is idolatry. Therefore, Jesus is Jehovah.

In Titus - In addition to the above, the Apostle Paul also makes a revealing statement when he writes to his beloved son Titus saying, "Looking for that blessed hope, and the glorious appearing of the great God and our Saviour Jesus Christ" (Titus 2:13). In this other passage,

Paul calls Christ "the Great God and Savior", but these titles have been reserved for the Lord since ancient times (Isaiah 43:10–11). Again, we must apply the questions asked in the previous subparagraph; and if we think there are two different gods, then we will be violating the rule of unity of writing. We have no choice but to recognize that "the great God and Savior" is indeed our Lord Jesus Christ.

In John - Finally, let us consider John's words and how he explains Jesus's relationship with God. "And we know that the Son of God is come, and hath given us an understanding, that we may know him that is true, and we are in him that is true, even in his Son Jesus Christ. This is the true God, and eternal life." (1 John 5:20). In this verse, just like the previous ones, John calls Jesus "the true God and eternal life". Let us note that the expression "the true God" highlights Jesus. Therefore, we can deduce in the same way as in the previous points, that Jesus is the same God of the Old Testament. The same God who said that outside of Him, there is no other God. Saying that, establishes that there is no other, and if there is no other, then we must accept Jesus Christ as the true God and eternal life.

Conclusion

We conclude this chapter by declaring that Jesus Christ is God and has all the attributes of the same God of the Old Testament. These attributes will be further elaborated to have a better understanding that Jesus Christ is the incarnated God who came to save the world from its sins. In addition, we have learned that if we understand the dual nature that was in Jesus, we can fully comprehend the texts which are difficult to interpret because of Jesus's Father-Son relationship with God.

Chapter 6

Jesus and the Triple Manifestation of God

≈

*And we know that the Son of God is come, and hath
given us an understanding, that we may know him that
is true, and we are in him that is true, even in his Son
Jesus Christ. This is the true God, and eternal life.*

1 JOHN 5:20

Perhaps one of the hardest things for a Christian is understanding the dynamics of Jesus in reference to the Father and the Holy Spirit. However, thanks to the explanation of the previous chapter on the dual nature of Jesus, it will be easier to understand what will be discussed in the present chapter.

In this section we will learn that in Jesus is the triple manifestation of God. In other words, Jesus is the Father, Jesus is the Son, and Jesus is the Holy Spirit.

Jesus and the Triple Manifestation of God

Earlier it was said that God's triple manifestation refers to the three common ways God has presented Himself to human beings. As a Father in creation (by creating all things), as a Son in redemption (by redeeming mankind), and as the Holy Spirit (in the lives of believers). However, in this chapter we will learn that these same manifestations of God as Father, as Son, and as Holy Spirit can be found in Jesus as well.

Jesus Claims to Be the Father

The Bible teaches that Jesus called Himself the Father on several occasions or at least that is what He tried to teach us. One of the Biblical passages that raised much controversy between the Jewish religious leaders and our Lord Jesus Christ, was undoubtedly when Jesus declares the following: "I and My Father are one" (John 10:30).

This has become known as Jesus's declaration as being the good shepherd and in response to the question of whether He was the Christ. Since Jesus replied in this manner, the religious leaders took stones to stone him, for they quickly understood that Jesus was calling Himself God the Father (John 10:33). However, this is not the only verse where He mentions this, just read chapter 14 of John.

A few verses before the aforementioned, Jesus had said: "I am the way, the truth, and the life: no man cometh unto the Father, but by me" (John 14:6). Apart from presenting Himself as the only way, the only truth, and the only life, He also presents Himself as someone who embodies the Father. In this passage, Jesus not only invites you to come to Him using the phrase, "No One Comes to the Father, but by me" where he clearly calls Himself the Father, but He also presents Himself as the only way to the Father.

Jesus also says in verse 7, "If ye had known me, ye should have known my Father also: and from henceforth ye know him and have seen him" (John 14:7). Jesus speaks of knowing and seeing the father; two very important points when meeting someone. One cannot know a person if one does not see them. That is why Jesus is said that if the disciples know Him and have seen Him, then they also know and have seen the Father. The one they were seeing with their own eyes was Jesus and not the Father. Someone can argue that Jesus is using this example in a symbolic way, however, the word "seen the Father" here actually refers to a physical form (we will clarify this later).

A third statement is given in verse 9, and this is even clearer than the previous ones. This is given when Philip does not yet understand and asks the Lord, "Lord, show us the Father, and it sufficeth us" (John 14:8). Jesus then answers saying, "Have I been so long time with you, and yet hast thou not known me, Philip? He that hath seen me hath seen the Father; and how sayest thou then, Show us the Father?" (John 14:9).

Again, the Master says to His disciples, but especially to Philip that seeing Jesus is seeing the Father. This is not symbolic but literal. In these, and in other verses, Jesus clearly tells his disciples that He is the Father. Obviously, this passage teaches us that Philip had not really understood who Jesus was yet; just as it is today. Many people have not yet understood who our Lord Jesus Christ is.

Finally, later in the same chapter we observe that Jesus lets them see even clearer that He is the Father; when He says to them, "I will not leave you comfortless (as orphans): I will come to you" (John 14:18). As their Father (not only in faith, but as God the Father) He would not leave them orphans but would always be with them. Thus, we conclude that Jesus claims to be the Father and those who had the privilege of seeing Him face to face, saw a revelation of God Himself in Jesus Christ.

To better understand the relationship of Jesus and the Father, I would like us to compare the actions of Jesus and the Father in the table below. It mentions three events in which both Jesus and the Father perform the same activity. Once read, we must answer the following: "Which one of the two (Father or Son) is doing such action? Or who should be attributed such an action?"

Table number 2		
Jesus	Action	Father
John 2:19–22	Who resurrects Jesus?	Romans 6:4
John 14:14	Who answers the prayer?	John 15:16
John 12:32	Who attracts people?	John 6:44

As can be seen in the table above, the same action is performed by both Jesus and the Father. Then, who should be attributed the action? Once the dual nature of Jesus has been understood, then it is not difficult to answer that in these three scenarios, both Jesus and the Father perform the same action because they are both the same person.

Jesus Claims to be the Son

The second manifestation of God and of Jesus is "the Son". Although we've already talked about this above, we must clarify here that the phrase "Son of God" when referring to Jesus appears a great number of times. However, we will only refer to a few occasions that are directly related to what we are explaining.

The angel said it to Mary in Luke 1:35. The angel used the phrase "Son of God" when he announced to Mary that she would be the mother of the redeemer.

His disciples also declared it when they saw His glory at sea (Matthew 14:33). These disciples not only said that He was the Son of God, but they also saw Him walk on the sea, and they witnessed how the wind and the storm were calmed by Him; and they worshipped Him.

Jesus Himself told the high priest in Matthew 26:63–64. This is undoubtedly the most important occasion of all the times the phrase "Son of God" is used to refer to the manifestation of God in the flesh. The high priest demanded an answer from Jesus. He said to Him, "I adjure thee by the living God, that thou tell us whether thou be the Christ, the Son of God." Imagine the scene: Israel's highest religious authority demands from Jesus an answer to the question that so many before him had previously asked and that no one could answer. Then comes the answer from the Master. Jesus saith unto him, "Thou hast said: nevertheless, I say unto you, Hereafter shall ye see the Son of man sitting on the right hand of power and coming in the clouds of heaven" (Matthew 26:63–64). We can see in this statement that Jesus gives

Himself the title "Son of God" when He is confronted under oath by the maximum authority of the Jews.

Finally, we must understand that this is the visible manifestation of God and, therefore, the most important in the process of the salvation of mankind. When God presents Himself as a man (Son) on this earth, all the prophecies that were written concerning God's plan to save mankind from his sins are fulfilled. Jesus Christ in His humanity was the only one who could go to the cross and die for us.

One of the problems that some Christians have is understanding all those times in which Jesus declares Himself as the son of man (or as the Son of God). However, when the dual nature of Jesus Christ has been understood, we have no problem. I recall a sentence from Dr. Fortino, when he said that to understand the divinity of Jesus, it is enough to ask oneself: "How is Jesus talking – as a man or like God?" If Jesus speaks as a man, then He is acting as a son, if He speaks like God, then He is the Father.

Jesus Claims to be the Holy Spirit

Finally, we have the manifestation of God as the Holy Spirit. As seen earlier Jesus manifests Himself to be the Father, but Jesus claims to be the Holy Spirit. We must clarify that, biblically speaking, this is the manifestation by which God leads His church after His departure from this world. We will explain this later, but for now we will only say that we are living under the dispensation of grace and the Holy Spirit is the one who rules and directs the church. To understand that Jesus is the Holy Spirit, let us discuss the following points:

1. There is only one Spirit.

Before proceeding with the explanation of the Holy Ghost, we must clarify that the Bible emphasizes that God is spirit and that there is only one Spirit.

There is one body, and one Spirit, even as ye are called in one hope
of your calling; One Lord, one faith, one baptism. Ephesians 4:4–5
This point is important because when God created man, He gave him
His spirit (breath) to live; and then, when Christ came to earth, He said
that His Spirit was going to live in mankind. We should not interpret
this as several spirits, but as Paul tells the Corinthians, "Now there are
diversities of gifts, but the same Spirit" (1 Corinthians 12:4).

2.   The Lord Jesus Christ is the Spirit.

We must understand that this Spirit is our Lord Jesus Christ. Let us
look at how Paul explains it in 2 Corinthians 3:17: "Now the Lord is
that Spirit: and where the Spirit of the Lord is, there is liberty." In this
verse, the word "Spirit" is associated with "Lord", therefore, we should
point out that "the Lord" in this case is the same as "the Spirit". This is a
direct revelation from God concerning Jesus because He called Himself
Lord in front of His disciples. This occurred when Jesus was giving
them a lesson about service and humility after washing their feet. He
said to them, "Ye call me Master and Lord: and ye say well; for so I am"
(John 13:13). Let us note that the disciples already called him master
and Lord, so, when He proclaimed Himself Lord, He also proclaimed
Himself as the Spirit – according to the Apostle Paul.

This is not an isolated case in which Jesus gives these revelations. On
another occasion, Jesus also states, "And I will pray the Father, and he
shall give you another Comforter, that he may abide with you forever;
Even the Spirit of truth; whom the world cannot receive, because it seeth
him not, neither knoweth him: but ye know him; for he dwelleth with
you, and shall be in you" (John 14:16–17).

In this biblical portion, we can discover several details. The first is that
the Father is to give the Comforter to the believers. This is the Holy
Spirit, whom the world cannot receive simply because it cannot see
him. Second, unlike the world, Jesus's disciples, know the Spirit. Now
the question is why is it that the disciples know the spirit? Because He

(Jesus) lives with them, but He will come and dwell within them, after He has ascended to heaven. This is a clear association of Jesus to the Holy Spirit. The term "it will be in you" simply means the fullness of the Holy Spirit. We will later explain the manifestation of the Holy Spirit in people, and the dwelling of the Spirit within Christians.

We conclude that Jesus has manifested himself as the Holy Spirit to his Church. It is interesting to consider two very important passages regarding this. The first is in John 16:7 where Jesus tells His disciples, "Nevertheless I tell you the truth; It is expedient for you that I go away: for if I go not away, the Comforter will not come unto you; but if I depart, I will send him unto you." In this verse we can observe a couple of points. The first point is in relation to what has been discussed. Jesus must go for the Spirit to come. The second has to do with dispensation – that is, the time of Jesus's manifestation as a Spirit. This cannot happen unless Jesus leaves. Someone may think that, if Jesus is God, he can also manifest Himself at the same time, and that is true. Nonetheless, what Jesus is referring to is the role the Holy Spirit would play after He has ascended to Heaven.

The second passage is found in John 14:18: "I will not leave you comfortless: I will come to you." The easiest way to interpret this verse is to say that Jesus as Father will not leave his children orphaned, however, the focus of this verse is that Jesus would not leave His children alone. This has to do with Jesus dwelling within them.

Dynamics of Jesus's Relationship with the Father and the Holy Spirit

One of the main problems that some Christians have in understanding that Jesus is God is pertaining to Christ's interaction with both the Father and the Holy Spirit. Many times, people do not understand this interaction, and they conclude that God is three different beings. To better understand this, we must ask ourselves the following:

1. Whose temple are we?

If the Father is a person, the Son is another person, and so is the Holy Spirit, who are we temples of? Since the Bible says the following:

- We are the temple of God (Father). (2 Corinthians 6:16)
- We are the temple of Christ. (2 Corinthians 13:5)
- We are a temple of the Holy Spirit. (1 Corinthians 6:19)

Anyone who understands that God has manifested himself in these three ways (Father, Son, and Holy Spirit), will not have a problem understanding that we are a temple of the same God.

2. Who raised Jesus from the dead?

If it is three people, then who raised Jesus from the dead? Since the Bible says the following:

- God raised him from the dead. (Acts 13:29–30)
- Jesus himself rose from the dead. (John 2:19)
- The Holy Spirit lifted Him from the dead. (Romans 8:11)

Anyone who has understood that God has manifested Himself in these three ways, doesn't have a problem understanding that Jesus rose Himself from the grave. We must understand the time and the occasion when Scripture is referring to this.

Jesus is the God Manifested in the Flesh

To conclude this, it is necessary to explain about the manifestation of God in the flesh. This was mentioned earlier, however, in this segment we will elaborate on it. Based on what we have presented before, God has manifested Himself to the world as Jesus Christ. In other words, the God who made the heavens and the earth came to this world in the flesh, that is, just like one of us. The most important thing about this statement is that the Bible itself confirms it. To do this, let's look at the following:

Jesus Himself declares it. When Jesus argues with the Jews about who the Father is, He says to them, "If ye had known me, ye should have known my Father also: and from henceforth ye know him, and have seen him" (John 14:7). In this verse we can see that Jesus emphasizes that knowing Him is to knowing God. The most significant thing is that He who has looked at Christ, has certainly looked at The Father. We must understand that this declaration is not symbolic sense or anything like that. The Lord is saying that whoever has seen Him, has seen the manifestation of God Himself in the flesh literally, that is Jesus Christ.

The Apostle John declares it. Another Biblical passage that declares that God became flesh is found in John. He says, "In the beginning was the Word, and the Word was with God, and the Word was God" (John 1:1). Also read John 1:14. This verse has been explained in hundreds of ways by various theologians to try to accommodate their way of thinking, however, we will try to look at it in the simplest way possible. This passage reveals that in the beginning of all things was the Word and that Word was with God and was God. We must be careful not to assume that they are two Words, or that the Word was another being that was with God, and that being was God. If we assume that there are two Words, it is automatically assuming that there was more than one God and that violates the rule of Oneness. Remember, God is one. However, John 1:1 cannot be disassociated from verse 14 of the same chapter. It says, "And the Word was made flesh, and dwelt among us" (John 1:14). This verse is a clear reference to Jesus Christ. That Word, who was God, became flesh and dwelt among us – and that is Jesus.

Paul also declares it. Finally, the Apostle Paul also makes his fundamental theological contribution by telling Timothy, "And without controversy great is the mystery of godliness: God was manifest in the flesh, justified in the Spirit, seen of angels, preached unto the Gentiles, believed on in the world, received up into glory" (1 Timothy 3:16).

This statement contains an impressive theological fact since it deals not only with the topic of the incarnation of God but also the identity of Jesus Christ, among other things. We can see that Paul clearly shows that God manifested Himself in the flesh as Jesus Christ. In addition, the verse is a clear reference to Christ Jesus.

It is Jesus who was manifested in the flesh; it is Jesus who was justified; it is Jesus who was seen by the angels; it is Jesus who was preached to the Gentiles; and it was Jesus who was received above in glory. Therefore, there is no doubt that the complete divinity is present in Jesus Christ, just as the Apostle Paul himself affirms. "For in him dwelleth all the fulness of the Godhead bodily." (Colossians 2:9)

We conclude that God's manifestation in the flesh, in the person of Jesus Christ, is the only way we could see and touch God. So, when Philip asks Jesus to show the father, Jesus scolds him by telling him that he has already seen the Father when he saw Him. (See John 14:7–10.)

Divine Attributes of Jesus

When we study Jesus Christ in relation to God, we can find several similarities between one and the other, especially when it comes to nature and attributes. There is a direct relationship between Jesus Christ and God Himself in what was mentioned above. This correlation clearly demonstrates that Jesus Christ is the same God of the Old Testament. To establish and test this theological posture, we must consider two very important things. First, the titles given to God and to Christ; and second, the attributes that both possess.

Jesus Holds the Same Titles as God

The following table presents a comparison between God and Jesus. It highlights which titles are given to God in Scripture and the titles given to Jesus - either by himself or by others.

Table number 3	
God is:	**Jesus is:**
The Rock: Deut. 32:1–4; 2 Sam. 22:3; Psalm 18:2; Isa. 17:10–11	The Rock; Mat. 16:17–19; Acts 4:11; 1 Cor. 10:4; Eph. 2:20; 1 Pet. 2:6
The One Who Comes: Ps. 50:1–6; Zac. 14:4–5; 1 Thess. 4:16; Rev. 19:11–16	The One Who Comes: Mat. 25:31–46; 1 Thess. 3:13; Titus 2:11–13
The Creator: Gen. 1: 1; Job 33:4; Psalm 33:6; Isa. 40:28; Mal. 2:10	The Creator: Jn. 1: 10; 1 Cor. 8:6
The Savior: Psalm 78:34–15; Psalm 10:21; Isa 43:3–11	The Savior: Luke 2:10–11; Acts 12:23; Phil. 3:20; 1 Tim. 4:10; Tit. 2:13
The Shepherd: Psalm 23:1, Psalm 100, Isa 40:11	The Shepherd: Jn. 10:11; Jn. 10:8–12; Heb. 13:20; 1 Pet. 2:25
The King: Psalm 44:4; Isa. 43:15; Jer. 10:10; Zac. 14:9	The King: Mt. 2:1–6; Luke 9:32–33; Jn. 18:37; 1 Tim. 6:13–16
The I Am: Ex. 3:14; Isa. 43:1–11	The I Am: Jn. 8:24–28; Jn. 18:5–8; Rev. 1:17–18
The First and the Last: Isa. 41:4; Isa 43:10–11; Isa. 44: 6–8	The First and the Last: Rev 1:8–11; Rev. 22:13

Jesus Christ Possesses the Same Attributes as God

In addition to the shared titles Jesus also possesses attributes that are only bestowed upon God. Let's look at only the most important ones:

1. Omnipotence. We have discovered that Jesus claimed to have "the omnipotence" of God on more than one occasion, however,

let us discuss the following: at the end of Jesus's ministry, He came to say, "All power is given unto me in heaven and in earth" (Matthew 28:18, Revelation 1:8, and John 17:2). This means, that all power was given to Him to do anything; this can only happen in the omnipotence of God. This is in addition to all the events in which Jesus Christ did powerful works that only God could do.

2. Omniscience. Another attribute we found in Jesus Christ is that He could know what was in a human without anyone telling Him anything. For example, He knew the thoughts of Simon the Pharisee when a sinful woman anointed his feet (Luke 7:36–47). When the Lord's disciples looked at examples like this, they came to say, "Now are we sure that thou knowest all things" (John 16:30). Read John 2:24–25 and John 4:16–19. God's Omniscience allowed Jesus Christ to have knowledge of anything.

3. Omnipresence. Omnipresence is the ability to be everywhere at the same time. One of the most powerful passages of scripture is found in John 3:13 when Jesus declares, "And no man hath ascended up to heaven, but he that came down from heaven, even the Son of man which is in heaven." If we carefully analyze the words of Jesus, we can see that He is saying that He can be everywhere at the same time. The verse speaks of the son of man, that is, Jesus in his human form. He can be in heaven and on earth at the same time. In Matthew 18:20, Jesus promises to always be with his disciples when they gather to worship Him.

Conclusion

In conclusion, we reiterate that God manifested himself as a man - Jesus Christ. That same spiritual God that no human had seen descended from heaven and became flesh just like humankind, so that we could touch Him and see Him. In addition, in this chapter we learned that

Jesus is not a smaller God or much less a God subordinate to the Father, Jesus Christ is the same Jehovah of the Old Testament, with all the titles and attributes of God. God became flesh to come to Earth and save us, because that was the only way the atonement of our sins would be fulfilled.

Chapter 7

The Man

≈

And God said, Let us make man in our image, after our likeness: and let them have dominion over the fish of the sea, and over the fowl of the air, and over the cattle, and over all the earth, and over every creeping thing that creepeth upon the earth. So God created man in his own image, in the image of God created he him; male and female created he them.

GENESIS 1:26–27

The existence of humans is and has been one of the most studied subjects by science and by all those who have tried to solve the mystery of its provenance. One of the biggest controversies about this subject is the famous theory of evolution, which states that humans descended from the monkey and that they have acquired their current status due to an evolutionary process. Myer explains it in a simple way: "The theory of evolution teaches us that all forms of life were born from one organism and that the higher species developed from the lower ones; so that, for example, the snail became a fish, the fish became a reptile, the reptile became a bird, and eventually, the monkey became human."[25]

However, we as Christians dismissed that theory because as Myer himself says: "God made the species distinct and separate, and placed an intermediate barrier so that, for example, a horse could not develop into a breed of animals that could no longer be named horses." That

[25] Myer Pearlman, *Teología Bíblica y Sistemática*, (Nashville, TN: Zondervan Editorial, 2013), 119.

is, they could not evolve. Myer also adds: "For example, the horse and the donkey belong to different species, because if they are crossed, they produce mules, and they are incapable of reproduction, that is, they cannot breed mules. This truth contradicts the theory of evolution, for it clearly demonstrates that God has placed a barrier that prevents one species from becoming another."[26]

In this chapter we will focus on explaining what the origin of mankind is, according to the scriptures and to a Christian worldview. In addition, we will learn some details of the way humans were created by God and what the purpose of His creation was. Finally, we will take a look at the dark side of humanity, focusing on the fall of mankind from the privileged place that God had given them since the day He formed them.

The Creation of Mankind

The Bible says that God is the creator of humans, and this contradicts all the beliefs and theories that man comes from the monkey or from any other form of creation. For a person who believes in God and in His word, this matter of the creation must be unquestionable. However, people who need an explanation that satisfies their thirst for a convincing answer, can find that answer in the sacred scriptures.

The Bible says that God is the creator of mankind. We'll look at some biblical portions that clearly emphasize it and explain a little bit about its meaning.

> So God created man in his own image, in the image of God created he him; male and female created he them. Genesis 1:27

In this verse we can appreciate that the creator of mankind is God; that God did it in His image (we will expand on this later); and finally, that God created them with a gender. He made a male and then a female. This has a core meaning in the establishment of humanity. By creating a

---

[26] Ibid. 121.

male and a female, God is setting the path for the reproduction and birth of future human beings. This was God's original plan, since a male and female are needed for human beings to reproduce.

> And the Lord God formed man of the dust of the
> ground, and breathed into his nostrils the breath of
> life; and man became a living soul. Genesis 2:7

The next element in the creation of man has to do with the way God made human beings which speaks to us about the greatness of the creator. Humans were formed from the dust of the earth. This means that God took the dirt and gave it the form that human beings now have. We can say without fear of being wrong, that God, with His own hands, formed each part of that dirt doll, exactly as He wanted.

> And the rib, which the Lord God had taken from man, made
> he a woman, and brought her unto the man. Genesis 2:22

The next element in God's creation was the making of the woman – the companion of the first man on earth. Interestingly, unlike the way he made the male, the female is made from one of the man's ribs. This fact is quite intriguing, as it reflects an intention of the creator for the human being. As the woman is made from the man's rib, it puts her in a special place in the life of the man, but also in a very different condition from the man. From there, we understand that the woman is a more fragile vessel (1 Peter 3:7).

> Know ye that the Lord he is God: it is he that hath
> made us, and not we ourselves; we are his people,
> and the sheep of his pasture. Psalms 100:3

Lastly, the Bible establishes God as the creator of mankind. Discarding that the human being has been created in any other way or much less the product of an evolutionary process or that humans themselves have had something to do with it. Therefore, the Christian must rule out any theory, opinion, or doctrine contrary to the above, since doing so would be rejecting God's work in creating the human being.

God Made Man in His Image and Likeness

The other matter to consider when we talk about the creation of man is: "How was it done?" The fundamental text for defining the creation of man is mentioned above and found in Genesis, when God said, "Let us make man in our image, after our likeness" (Genesis 1:26). Humans were not only created by God, but they were created in His likeness. The word likeness comes from alike and the academy of the Spanish language translates it as, "the resemblance of someone or something; compares to; the same as or different in size, but having equal parts in proportion. Therefore, man resembles God or has a resemblance to God.[27]

God has given humans something that no one else could – His image. It must be understood that the image of God does not refer to a physical appearance, or similar in face or figure, for God is spirit (John 4:24) and man is human, rather it refers to a spiritual and moral image. Humans inherited from God all that is good, pure, just, and anything that has to do with high morality. It must be ruled out that man looks like God physically.

God Made Mankind with Unique Characteristics

Unlike animals, humans were made with the hands of God, and of course God put unique qualities in them that make them totally different from the other beings of creation. Here we notice three characteristics that humans possessed from the day they were created.

Humans Possess Intellectual Faculties

The first man on earth possessed intellectual faculties that the animals of creation did not have. The biblical verse says of this the following: "And out of the ground the Lord God formed every beast of the field, and every fowl of the air; and brought them unto Adam to see what he

---

[27] Rae.es, "semejanza", http://dle.rae.es/?id=XVv80p3. Retrieved 24 July, 2019.

would call them: and whatsoever Adam called every living creature, that was the name thereof" (Genesis 2:19).

God gave humans the ability to reason, think, and the creativity to name all the animals that God had created. This ability is the source of all scientific knowledge. The mind of the human being is the greatest thing one can possess, since with their minds humans can create, envision, and think. In the mind of the individual there is a source of knowledge and wisdom – this is something only God could do. It is worth mentioning that this is another area in which humans have the image of God, since equally God is a super intelligent being.

Humans Possess a Holy Moral Nature

The other significant aspect of the human being is that it was made with an exceptional condition. Humans were created pure and holy, that is, without sin. These are also the traits of the Highest God who dwells in holiness and is a pure God. These are the conditions in which humans were created. The Bible says, "Lo, this only have I found, that God hath made man upright; but they have sought out many inventions" (Ecclesiastes 7:29). In the beginning, the first man enjoyed the greatest blessing of being clean. This was nothing more than the reflection of God who had created a being like Him, for God dwells in holiness. Unfortunately, that joy of holiness did not last long in the human being.

Humans were Created Innocent

Finally, the human being was created innocent and without any malice. Such was the innocence in them that they did not identify the trap that the enemy was setting on them, since they were naked and did not realize it. Innocence is the purest aspect an individual can have. One can observe this in young children. When someone offers them a treat in exchange for a $20 bill they quickly agree without any hesitation because he does not know the value of that $20 bill. This is what human beings were like in the beginning.

God Made Humans for a Purpose

Just how everything God does has a purpose, so was the creation of mankind. The idea of creating man was not random, let alone without purpose. God was clear about the reason for their creation and existence. In this section we will discuss God's purpose in creating man on earth.

God Made Man to Have Communion with Him

One of God's great purposes in creating humans was to have an intimate relationship with them. God was making someone with whom He could engage in communication and establish an intimate relationship. Although God had many angels and created beings in Heaven to have communion with, He found something special in humans that angelic beings did not have. Humans have a will and a special need, which the angels did not have. Humans, like God, also need an intimate relationship. Human beings were created by the great love of God, and He did it to have a relationship with them, so much so that the world itself was created so God could share it with man (Ephesians 1:4–5).

God Made Humans to Manifest His Nature

Another purpose for which God made mankind was to manifest His nature in him. Humans enjoy spiritual privileges that the angels themselves do not possess. For example, it is humans whom God calls His children; it is humans for whom He came to save and for whom He gave his life on the cross. It is to humans He has given of His love and mercy. It is humans who have been given a mind and a heart like God's (e.g., David. 1 Samuel 2:35).

We do not see that God has done such a thing for the angels. Moreover, it is to humans that God has given the greatest gift – His spirit. First, at creation when God blew the breath of life unto him; and second, once converted to God, humans receive the gift of the Holy Spirit. For this reason, the psalmist could not bear so much blessing that he burst into exclamation:

> What is man, that thou art mindful of him? and the son of man, that thou visitest him? For thou hast made him a little lower than the angels, and hast crowned him with glory and honour. Psalms 8:4–5

In this exclamation, David demonstrates the privileged place that human beings have compared to angels.

God Made Humans to Share His Government

If that is not enough, the human being received a portion of authority from God. They were given the responsibility to rule and govern over the beasts of the field and over the earth itself. The Psalmist continues with this eloquent exclamation:

> Thou madest him to have dominion over the works of thy hands; thou hast put all things under his feet: All sheep and oxen, yea, and the beasts of the field; The fowl of the air, and the fish of the sea, and whatsoever passeth through the paths of the seas. Psalms 8:6–8

Humans rule over God's creation. By the grace of God we have received a great privilege: God has shared His government with human beings. Imagine what the Apostle Peter felt when Jesus said to him:

> And I will give unto thee the keys of the kingdom of heaven: and whatsoever thou shalt bind on earth shall be bound in heaven: and whatsoever thou shalt loose on earth shall be loosed in heaven. Matthew 16:19

If we consider these words, we probably say, "This is too much power for a mortal man." However, that is what God did with humans, simply to show His great love for us.

God Made Man to Fulfill His Purpose

God made man to fulfill God's purposes for this earth and for His creation. In other words, although God does not need help, He made mankind to "help" Him carry out His works and projects of establishing His kingdom here on earth.

> And God blessed them, and God said unto them, Be fruitful,
> and multiply, and replenish the earth, and subdue it: and have
> dominion over the fish of the sea, and over the fowl of the air, and
> over every living thing that moveth upon the earth. Genesis 1:28

So it is mankind who received the privilege of governing creation on behalf of God and received the mission of carrying out the plans of the Almighty for this humanity. We are appointed collaborators of God (1 Corinthians 3.9) because we are committed to a mission that He has given us, and we must carry it out as He planned.

God Gave Humans Free Will

Perhaps the greatest thing of all is that God made humans with the ability to decide. This is what is best known as "free will". God did not make humans like robots but gave them a will of their own.

Humans had the ability and freedom to choose what was best for themselves and what they wanted to do. God, in His great love, doesn't impose anything on anyone by force, although He may well do so, but God's chivalry is so great that He gave humans the freedom to choose. That is why one of the most important biblical passages is found in Deuteronomy 30:19. It says: "I call heaven and earth to record this day against you, that I have set before you life and death, blessing and cursing: therefore choose life, that both thou and thy seed may live."

Unfortunately, as we already know, mankind chose the wrong path and that had serious consequences, which we will see later. However, it is worth mentioning this to all those who complain often that their life is going wrong and complain to God about all the bad things. In reality, they can only blame themselves for they are responsible for their own decisions and actions.

The Fall of Mankind

One of the saddest and most painful things we find in the Bible is the fall of mankind from the privileged place that God had given them. Everything they were and had suddenly comes down and everything collapses. From one moment to the next, they lost all that they had received and went from the light to the darkness. Mankind fell from God's grace and became an ordinary human being. In this section we will briefly discuss the subject of the fall and focus on three areas of study

- What caused the fall?
- How was the fall?
- What were the consequences of the fall?

What caused the fall?

When studying the fall of mankind, the first question that arises is, "Why did it happen? Or what caused it?" So, we must focus our study on the reason of the fall, that is, what caused mankind to fall from grace. Although we can delve deeply into the subject, the answer is summed up in a simple sentence: "Mankind fell because they disobeyed God." The fall was due to the disobedience of God's commandment.

Even though God's commandment and instruction was simple, in comparison to what we know today about sin, nonetheless, breaking that commandment caused humans to fail.

And the Lord God commanded the man, saying, Of every tree of the garden thou mayest freely eat: But of the tree of the knowledge of good and evil, thou shalt not eat of it: for in the day that thou eatest thereof thou shalt surely die. Genesis 2:16–17

We can understand through this passage that God's commandment was simple and not complicated (at least for us). God's directive was that they should not eat the fruit that grew on the tree of the knowledge of good and evil. We must clarify that the forbidden fruit was not an apple, or much less sexual intercourse as some suggest, but it was the fruit of the tree of good and evil.

The phrase of "good and evil" is simply interpreted as this: in that particular tree, God had put the knowledge of good and evil. In other words, God already knew that they were going to eat from it, therefore that tree was like a key to open the understanding of what was good and bad. Furthermore, this was a special tree placed on God's side in the garden exclusively to test man. The command was simple and straightforward: they should not eat that fruit and that's it.

The Temptation

The second element is precisely the strategy that was used in the fall, which is what we call "temptation". The Bible is clear in defining not only the temptation, but the tempter as well.

Now the serpent was more subtle than any beast of the field which the Lord God had made. And he said unto the woman, Yea, hath God said, Ye shall not eat of every tree of the garden? Genesis 3:1

In this biblical passage we can discover at least three fundamental points that come to light in temptation.

- First, the identity of the tempter. In this case, the tempter is the serpent, who is a clear manifestation of the devil himself, who uses the snake as an instrument to be able to speak to the woman.

- Second, the person that was tempted. The woman was tempted by the ancient serpent that is the devil and Satan according to Revelation 12:9, which was already in operation from the beginning.
- Finally, how this temptation took place. The tempter spoke to the woman, and she listened to his words.

Notice that the devil twists the words God had given to them. God had told them, "You can eat from every tree, except from the tree of good and evil." Yet the devil said unto them, "Yes, has God said, you shall not eat of every tree of the garden?" We can already see that the devil was beginning to carry out his evil plan and did not miss the opportunity that the woman was giving him: her having paid attention and hearing his misleading words.

Temptation is one of the strategies that Satan has used from the beginning. The reason is that through this instrument, mankind can be seduced and fall, as Adam and Eve did. The devil uses the individual's senses such as sight, mind, and feelings to seduce and case a fall.

The Fall

The third element in the fall of Adam and Eve has to do with the failure of mankind itself. The reason for this importance is that it is a very significant event in the history of humanity. On one hand it establishes human nature with its frailties and, on the other hand, the devil's astuteness to deceive.

> And when the woman saw that the tree was good for food, and that it was pleasant to the eyes, and a tree to be desired to make one wise, she took of the fruit thereof, and did eat, and gave also unto her husband with her; and he did eat. Genesis 3:6

Let us note the development that led to the fall of the first humans in the garden of Eden. First, the woman was Satan's victim, for the tempter came to her, showing her how good and beneficial the forbidden tree was. Second, she saw that the tree was good and pleasing to the eyes and it was also a means to attain wisdom. Those were the words the enemy sowed in her heart. Third, she ate the forbidden fruit; and fourth, she gave the fruit to her husband to eat too. That is how they both fell into the devil's trap.

When mankind disobeyed God, they fell from God's grace and the privileged place God had given them. When they fell, that glory that God had placed in them also fell and sin was consummated. They had simply failed God and the first thing they did was hide from God, for they felt ashamed of themselves.

> And the eyes of them both were opened, and they
> knew that they were naked; and they sewed fig leaves
> together, and made themselves aprons. Genesis 3:7

The other issue to consider in the fall is that, from that moment on, they lost the innocence they had, for their eyes were opened, and they were able to know good and evil, as God had told them. Something interesting in this scene is that they realized they were naked, although they were always naked, however, it wasn't until they sinned that they realized it. This is a clear revelation that they had lost their innocence.

Some considerations of the Fall

1.   Mankind fell by their own decision.

God made humans so perfect that it was that same perfection that gave them the decision to sin or not to sin. Although they had the evil influence of Satan to sin, they could have resisted, yet God had given them the ability to decide, whether or not to do so. The human being has always had that ability to decide whether to do good or wrong, yet in this case, the first humans decided to do wrong.

2.   God had nothing to do with the fall.

It is important to mention that God had nothing to do with the fall, much less allowed them to sin. We must emphasize again that humans made this decision to do so, for God will never allow sin, let alone tolerate it. Although God knows and understands all things, it was entirely their decision.

3.   There are consequences of disobedience.

When God discovered their sin, He brought judgment upon them and the tempter, and He gave His punishment to each of them. Sin brought irreparable consequences in the lives of all involved.

The serpent received his punishment. "Thou art cursed above all cattle, and above every beast of the field; upon thy belly shalt thou go, and dust shalt thou eat all the days of thy life" (Genesis 3:14). The serpent was the instrument that Satan used to tempt the woman, and God punished it, as God punishes every being who lets themselves be used by the devil. Some suggest that before the fall, snakes did not crawl like they do today.

The woman received her punishment. "I will greatly multiply thy sorrow and thy conception; in sorrow thou shalt bring forth children" (Genesis 3:16). From that moment on, the woman received the punishment of enduring the strongest physical pain that a human being can experience in the body. Giving birth causes the woman to suffer a great amount, before, during, and even after childbirth. One of the reasons given by God may be for her to remember her sin, each pain is a memory that she failed God.

The man also received his punishment. "Because thou hast hearkened unto the voice of thy wife, and hast eaten of the tree, of which I commanded thee, saying, Thou shalt not eat of it: cursed is the ground for thy sake; in sorrow shalt thou eat of it all the days of thy life" (Genesis 3.17). It is curious that when He reaches the man, God does not curse him like the serpent, but on the contrary, he curses the earth. Once again showing God's great love for human beings. Some suggest that the reason is because the man had been created in the image of God and that is why He turns His curse against the earth, from which man was precisely taken.

Mankind is banished from the garden.

> Therefore the Lord God sent him forth from the garden of
> Eden, to till the ground from whence he was taken. So he
> drove out the man; and he placed at the east of the garden of
> Eden Cherubims, and a flaming sword which turned every
> way, to keep the way of the tree of life. Genesis 3:23–24

The judgment for the human being was carried out by God and they were cast out of His presence. The Bible says that humans, because of sin, lost a lot. they lost the image of God in themselves. They lost that beauty and honor, and they became miserable, separated from God. In addition, they lived without the privileges they had before and were cast from the garden of Eden and had to work the land and struggle to feed themselves.

But, perhaps the most terrible thing, was living far from the presence of God. This is exactly what sin does in humans, it separates them from God's presence. From then on, mankind was in a very bad condition.

Conclusion

We conclude this chapter, mentioning that the history of mankind's creation is very fascinating, but also very sad because of the fall. However, it didn't end there! Later, we will study how God helped humans get out of the hole they were in.

We hope that this chapter has helped to understand the place of glory that mankind had and the great loss that sinning caused. I hope this helps us learn to value what we have received from God, learn to care for it, and that we can learn to obey God above anything.

Chapter 8

Sin

≈

And the Lord said, Because the cry of Sodom and Gomorrah
is great, and because their sin is very grievous.

GENESIS 18:20

Sin was one of the elements that led man to his spiritual bankruptcy; it is very important to study it to understand its theological and spiritual implications. Thus, we must begin this chapter by asking a couple of questions on this sensitive subject. The first should be, "What does the Bible really teach about sin? And second, "What do we truly believe and accept from the doctrine of sin?"

In today's world, it is necessary to define sin because, as time goes on, the confusion becomes more palpable as different philosophical thoughts, religious currents, and various medias do their job. In a society where it is very easy to convey opinions, concepts, and even sinful acts, it is imperative that the church defines its position before a society that classifies things daily from a human perspective and far from what God teaches through His holy word.

Josh McDowell writes that we are on the verge of immorality and claims that many young people on various occasions have often lied to their parents, teachers, classmates. They've watched inappropriate TV shows, broken school rules, smoked cigarettes, used drugs, or gotten drunk; but perhaps most surprisingly, more than 50% of young people have groped someone or have had sex and their parents haven't even been made aware of it.[28]

In this chapter we will try to define sin, considering the sacred scriptures, as well as some theological concepts about it. In addition, we will learn about the origin of sin and its influence on human beings.

Some Definitions of Sin

To better understand the meaning of sin, we should first study some definitions to have a broader idea of what we want to say. The reason is simple, as mentioned in the introduction, perhaps what sin means for one, may be different for someone else. Therefore, based on that way of thinking, a complete definition of sin is necessary.

Word Definitions

1. The Royal Academy of the Language translates the word sin as follows. Sin is a word that comes from the Latin, "peccatum" and may have the following applications:

    a. Voluntary transgression of religious precepts.
    b. A thing that departs from the right and just, or that is missing what is due.
    c. Excess or defect on any line.[29]

Based on that, sin is defined as a voluntary transgression of some established law, and it departs from what is right and good by those who participate in it.

2. For the Greeks, the word sin comes from the word "hamartia" and can be translated as: "failure of the goal, not hitting the

---

[28] Josh McDowell, *Es bueno o Es malo,* (El Paso, TX: Editorial Mundo Hispano, 1996), 19-20.
[29] *Real Academia Española,* (Madrid, Espa2006).

target". This is a phrase commonly used in Christian circles. Although this word has a lighter connotation, it still has its negative implications. However, it softens the contents of the definition.

3. The Larousse dictionary translates it as "transgression of divine law". Here we can see that this translation gives you a theological approach because sin actually has a theological implication and is not just a matter of doing something bad in relation to the good.[30]

4. The dictionary of Theological Terms defines it as follows: "It is the fundamental lack of belief, mistrust and rejection of God and of the human displacement of God as the center of reality".[31]

5. Some other translations of Strong's etymological dictionary and biblical concordance are as follows:

    a. Kjataá. It means an offense. (Genesis 20:9)
    b. Asham. It translates as guilt. (Genesis 26:10)
    c. Avon. It translates as perversity. (Exodus 28:43)
    d. Kjatá. It means to miss. (Leviticus 5:1)
    e. Hamartia. Also, like Kjatá, is missing the mark. (Matthew 1: 21, 2:5, 2:7)
    f. Paraptoma. Translates as error or transgression. (Ephesians 1:7)
    g. Agnome. This word translates as weakness or frailty. (Hebrews 9:7)[32]

The Concept of Sin

For Christianity, sin is the separation of mankind from the will of God, which appears collected in the sacred books (the Bible). When people violate some of the divine commandments, they commit a sin.

---

[30] *El pequeño Larousse Ilustrado*, (Mexico City: Edition Larousse, 2005).

[31] Stanley J. Grenza, David Guretzki y Cherith Fee Nordling. *Términos teológicos*, (El Paso, TX: Editorial Mundo Hispano, 2006).

[32] James Strong. *Nueva Concordancia Strong Exhaustiva*, (Nashville, TN 2002).

The use of the term sin is not exclusive to religious people, although in the case of atheists and agnostics there is usually a much lower degree of understanding of the characteristics and consequences of an offense of this nature. In fact, for those who do not embrace any religion, it is possible to use this word with total lightness, even in a mocking tone, while a Christian, for example, knows in detail the weight and content of the concept.

A sin must be distinguished from a crime: sin disappoints God, as the creator of life and crime, on the other hand, implies the breach of a series of rules established by the human being. Although the same action can fall into both classifications if the person responsible is a religious person, not only will they have to pay the penalty decided by a judge, but they will suffer for having failed their highest authority, God, and that will weigh much more than worldly suffering.

Outside of the religious sphere, certain excesses or defects are usually considered as sins. For example, it is said that wasting food is a sin, since we live on the same planet as the millions of people who starve to death.

The Origin of Sin

Perhaps the greatest unknown question of all time concerning sin is, "Where did sin originate?" or "Why are people so evil? Whether we choose to accept it or not, the general population oftentimes does not understand the reality of sin or evil nature. However, the Bible can answer this. Although this subject was briefly discussed in the previous chapter, it is necessary to elaborate on the theological and eschatological consequences of sin.

Sin Does Not Come from God

Some people, in their frustration, blame God for everything that happens to them and have even dared to say that God is responsible for all their downfalls, but that is not the case. Foremost, it must be understood that sin does not come from God, nor did He create it. A few of the writers and men in the Bible give mention to the relationship between God and sin.

For example, Job went so far as to say, "Far be it from God, that he should do wickedness; and from the Almighty, that he should commit iniquity" (Job 34:10). The prophet Isaiah said, "Holy, holy, holy, is the Lord" (Isaiah 6:3). Moses said, "A God of truth and without iniquity, just and right is he" (Deuteronomy 32:4).

God said himself, "And ye shall be holy unto me: for I the Lord am holy" (Leviticus 20:26). When He appeared to Moses in the middle of the bush, He commanded him saying, "Put off thy shoes from off thy feet, for the place whereon thou standest is holy ground" (Exodus 3:5).

God is a holy God and sin, ungodliness, and wickedness are far from His presence. Therefore, He could not have created sin. When He created man, He made him clean, pure and without blemish and gave a resemblance of Himself. God created man in His image and likeness, as mentioned in the previous chapter.

Louis Berkhof says, "God cannot be regarded as the author of sin." He also adds, "Truly God hates sin."[33] From here stems another point of important relevance – the permissive action of God that goes hand in hand with the thought we have often heard: "Why did God allow sin?" Or, "If God knew that man was going to fail, why did He allow it?" The truth of it all is that God did not allow sin but rather gave mankind the ability to choose, and they chose to sin.

Sin Began in the Spiritual World

Although we often refer to the beginning of sin as the sin of Adam and Eve, we must recognize that sin occurred long before that. Sin began with Satan's rebellion in heaven, when he wanted to be equal to God,

---

[33] Lyes Berkhof, *Teología sistemática*, (Jeninson, MI:T.E.L.L. 1995), 261-262.

deceived many angels, and took them with him. Although the time frame of this rebellion is not well known, we at least know a few facts. For example, when Jesus said of the devil that "He was a murderer from the beginning" (John 8:44). In a separate passage, the Apostle John says, "For the devil sinneth from the beginning" (1 John 3:8). This principle must be understood as being the beginning of earthly things and even of mankind itself.

So, sin began with the devil, or "in the spiritual world", because it occured in that immaterial world, which human beings cannot see, and at the beginning of time. The Apostle John says of this in 1 John 3:7–8, "Little children, let no man deceive you: he that doeth righteousness is righteous, even as he is righteous. He that committeth sin is of the devil; for the devil sinneth from the beginning."

The influence of the devil is so great that humans sin and it has been like this from the beginning. This "principle" is explained well by Matthew Henry in his commentary. He says, "The devil is in a constant attitude of sin, and this principle does not refer to time or when the devil was created, but rather from the moment he rebelled against God, and that is where he began to be a devil.[34]

The prophet Ezekiel sheds even more light on this case when he says:

How art thou fallen from heaven, O Lucifer, son of the morning! how art thou cut down to the ground, which didst weaken the nations! For thou hast said in thine heart, I will ascend into heaven, I will exalt my throne above the stars of God: I will sit also upon the mount of the congregation, in the sides of the north: I will ascend above the heights of the clouds; I will be like the most High. Yet thou shalt be brought down to hell, to the sides of the pit. Isaiah 14:12–15

When Satan was cast out after he sinned and rebelled against God, he began to influence humanity with the same nature that characterizes

---

[34] Mattew Henry, *Comentario bíblico, traducido y adaptado por Francisco Lacueva*, (Terrassa, Barcelona: Editorial Clie, 1999), 1888.

him. Then, powered by his wickedness and being full of pride and vanity, Satan turned to the earth to empty all the poison he brought with him and initiated a great rebellion against the Creator. Thus, making known his malevolent nature and giving himself the title of the father of lies and the author of all sin.

Sin and Its Impact on Mankind

As mentioned in the previous chapter, the first parents (Adam and Eve) were tempted by the devil to disobey God causing sin to infiltrate humanity. Sin had a great impact on their lives. Because of this, they suffered a considerable change in their lives and in other areas of their existence.

Sin Affected Their Person and Their Being

Sin affects a person's spirit, soul, body, conscience, and emotions. When Adam and Eve had sinned, they realized they were naked and covered themselves (Genesis 3:7). They were afraid of God and hid from Him. Undoubtedly, they now had a fear of the Holy God because their eyes were opened to understand the difference between them and God – between their sinfulness and the holiness of God.

Sin Affected God's Image in Them

Although there are variances in this sentiment, it is generally accepted that after sinning, mankind lost the image of God within. Some experts, like Luther, argue that they lost God's image completely, while others say that it only deteriorated or diminished.

Francisco Lacueva explains it as follows: "Due to sin, the image of God was deteriorated, but not completely erased." He adds, "They lost communion with God, fleeing from Him; but they did not know themselves either, ashamed of their own body and feeling within themselves the rebellion of instincts."[35] They were no longer the same. Now, the image of God in them was stained, affected, and deteriorated.

Sin Affected Their Relationship with God

When they were cast out of Paradise, they were also cast out of God's presence. Therefore, the relationship that humans had with God was also affected, for sin creates a great separation between God and mankind. The Bible says of this in Generis, "Therefore the Lord God sent him forth from the garden of Eden, to till the ground from whence he was taken" (Genesis 3:23) and adds, "So He drove out the man" (Genesis 3:24).

The biblical commentator Matthew Henry says it this way, "His relationship with God was repealed and lost, and that communication that had been established between man and his maker was interrupted."[36]

It is important to emphasize that the most significant impact that mankind had in sinning was the severance of their relationship with God. As explained in the previous chapter, God had created humans to have intimacy with Him and to live in communion with Him; however, when they fell, that longed-for communion was lost.

Sin Affected Their Eternal Future

One of the greatest effects of eschatological proportions that sinning caused was the fact that man was also separated from God eternally. Although we will expand on this thought later, it is worth mentioning that one of the most serious effects of sin is that it can send the individual to eternal damnation if nothing is done to remedy it. The Bible says of this, "For all have sinned, and come short of the glory of God" (Romans 3:23).

---

[35] Francisco Lacueva, *Ética Cristiana,* (Barcelon, Spain: Editorial Clie, 1975), 128.
[36] Mattew Henry, Op. cit. 24.

When mankind sinned, not only had it caused for them to be kicked out of the garden of Eden, but it had also opened the doors for their own eternal damnation. Sin brings separation from God and death, as the Bible itself says, "For the wages of sin is death; but the gift of God is eternal life through Jesus Christ our Lord" (Romans 6:23). By sinning, their eternal future was at stake, but God, in His sovereignty, had established a way to free humans from that destiny.

Conclusion

We conclude this chapter by mentioning that sin is a cancer in the human being. However, the greatest part of this is knowing that God did not remain silent. He gave the solution to deal with sin and provided His salvation, as we will see in the next chapter. "But God commendeth his love toward us, in that, while we were yet sinners, Christ died for us" (Romans 5:8). The Lord Jesus Christ himself says, "For the Son of man is come to seek and to save that which was lost" (Lucas 19:10).

Chapter 9

The Plan of Salvation

≈

For God so loved the world, that he gave his only begotten Son, that whosoever believeth in him should not perish, but have everlasting life.

JOHN 3:16

In the previous chapter we learned that human beings fell from God's grace because of sin and that they were condemned to death because of their sin. But God did not want to leave him there, but decided to save him, so he devised a plan to do it. That plan is called, "salvation".

The topic of salvation is very important in Christianity, since in it we can see the love and work of God at its finest. Moreover, it is of utmost importance for it to be understood by all Christians, as it reminds us of where Christ brought and delivered us from.

I believe that we have all spoken about or heard of salvation at some point in our lives. I believe that most people have hope for the salvation of their soul. That is why the study of salvation must undoubtedly be one of the most important points of Christianity. It should also be one of the greatest concerns for every child of God. Therefore, in this chapter we will study the need for salvation, what God has saved us from, and what are the requirements are to attain salvation.

The Need for Salvation

To understand the topic of salvation, it is necessary to ask some fundamental questions, such as:

- What is salvation?
- Why do we need salvation?
- What must we do to be saved?

If someone does not understand the need for salvation, it will be almost impossible for that person to seek salvation.

Why do we need salvation? Perhaps the obvious question for anyone interested must be, "Why is salvation needed?" The need for salvation begins with understanding that the wages of sin are death. This is what the Bible teaches.

> For the wages of sin is death; but the gift of God is eternal
> life through Jesus Christ our Lord. Romans 6:23

In other words, sin produces not only destruction, but death and doom as well. Death must first be understood as physical death, but it also has eschatological repercussions, or eternal consequences. Primarily, we must be saved from death.

The other matter to consider is in correlation with the condemnation of the individual's soul. There is a very sad truth: the end for the sinner will be eternal damnation. Our Lord Jesus Christ made it very clear when He came to this world and announced the following regarding the future:

> For the hour is coming, in the which all that are in the graves
> shall hear his voice, And shall come forth; they that have done
> good, unto the resurrection of life; and they that have done
> evil, unto the resurrection of damnation. John 5:28–29

Although we will expand on this point later, it is worth mentioning that a day will come when all people must appear before God to account for their actions, whether good or bad. If they were good, they will receive the reward of eternal life and if they were evil, then they will receive condemnation.

The Reality of Life

There is a reality that we cannot avoid, as much as we want to: one day we will die, for we are not eternal in this world. The Bible says that man is like the flower of the field, which comes out in the morning and is no more in the evening (Psalm 103:15-16). But there is another reality, which is that life does not end when we die, but quite the contrary, it is where eternity begins. Therefore, if our behavior was good, we will enjoy salvation, but if it was evil, then condemnation awaits us.

Where do the dead go? Even though dying may not be a problem, the more obvious question would be, "Where are the dead going?" We've always heard comments about people's future when they die. There are people who believe that when someone dies, they go to the grave and that's where it all ends. Others believe that they are going somewhere in between, but the truth is, that is not the case either. The Bible has the answer to this question. The sacred writer puts it this way: "All go unto one place; all are of the dust, and all turn to dust again" (Ecclesiastes 3:20). He adds, "Then shall the dust return to the earth as it was: and the spirit shall return unto God who gave it" (Ecclesiastes 12:7).

We must establish that man is a threefold being, composed of body, soul, and spirit. Although this vision of the human being may vary according to religious tradition, in most cases, Christians agree that the human being is composed of three parts. When you die, each part of you goes to a different place, as explained below.

• The body goes to the grave.

According to Ecclesiastes 12:7 the body goes to the grave, that is, to the earth which is where it came from. Hence the Christian practice is of burying the dead since it usually does not contemplate cremation or any other practice.

- The spirit goes to God.

According to the same passage from Ecclesiastes 12:7, the spirit returns to God who gave it. This spirit is that breath of life that God gave when we were made from the dust of the earth. That breath of life usually returns to God. A curious fact is that when Christ was on the cross of the Cavalry and came to an end here on earth, the Bible says that He "delivered the spirit" (Matthew 27:50 and John 19:30).

- The soul goes where it belongs.

Finally, the soul goes where it belongs. The soul must be understood as the true individual, and therefore, the eternal part of the human being. Most agree that the soul is the result of the union of the body and the spirit. According to the Bible there are only two places where the souls of the dead go; at least this is what Jesus established. Jesus said, "For the hour is coming, in the which all that are in the graves shall hear his voice, And shall come forth; they that have done good, unto the resurrection of life; and they that have done evil, unto the resurrection of damnation" (John 5:28–29).

It is necessary to establish that there are two places reserved for humans, which have been traditionally defined as heaven and hell. At this point we will thoroughly clarify these concepts, since the Bible also speaks of the lake of fire as the final punishment of the wicked.

To better understand the future of humans after death, Jesus uses a parable, which clearly explains a few of the details about what happens after death. This is the parable of the rich man and Lazarus, found in Luke 16:19-31. In this parable the Lord Jesus illustrates in detail the process of a human's life and how things will be after death, so that we may have an idea.

There are Only Two Places

The parable of the rich man and Lazarus speaks of two men with different fates in the world. The rich man would throw many parties, while the beggar stood at his door begging and trying to eat what the rich man threw away. However, one day they both died since death does not discriminate between the rich and the poor.

The interesting thing about the story is that the beggar dies and was carried by the angels to Abraham's bosom. Curiously, and simultaneously, the rich man also dies, and was buried. We immediately learn from the account of Jesus, that the big difference begins here. While the rich man is buried, the beggar was carried by the angels to Abraham's bosom.

One of the verses in the parable illustrates the two places and the condition in which they are found. "And in hell he lift up his eyes, being in torments, and seeth Abraham afar off, and Lazarus in his bosom" (Luke 16:23).

Here we can see that Jesus speaks of two places. Abraham's bosom and Hades.

1. The bosom of Abraham. This is the place where the souls of the righteous went in the Old Testament, before the resurrection of our Lord Jesus Christ.
2. Hades. This place literally means: the region of lost spirits. This word is written in Greek and is the transliteration of the Hebrew word Seol, which means insatiable. It was considered in the Old Testament as a place of oblivion for the wicked. Hades in Greek has been translated as grave, hell, abyss, etc. It is believed, from the biblical account, that the Seol contained both the abyss where the unjust were and the bosom of Abraham in the upper part where the righteous were. It was precisely to that place that the beggar was taken.

The characteristics of each place.

It is important to emphasize that Jesus shows us not only the future of these two individuals but the characteristics of each place where both are located. Hades was a place of torment, while Abraham's bosom was a resting place.

We can learn from the story that the rich man was in torment (v. 23), thirsty and in a flame (v.24) while the beggar was comforted (v. 25). In other words, each had gone to the place where they belonged to receive what they each deserved.

The time when these things happen.

The other element to consider is the time in which things happen. With this parable, Jesus refutes the popular belief of a place called purgatory where souls go for an allotted time to be purified. It should be noted that according to the parable of the rich man and Lazarus, after the two men died, they immediately went to their corresponding place. This tells us that God does not delay His word regarding this.

There is also another instance in the Bible in reference to the two places where the souls of humans go after they die and at the time these things happen. When Jesus was crucified, there were two thieves crucified with Him, one on each side, and while one of them blasphemed, the other cried out to Jesus and said, "Lord, remember me when thou comest into thy kingdom" (Luke 23:42).

We can see that this thief repented at the last moment and cried out for mercy to Jesus. Christ then answered him saying, "Today shalt thou be with me in paradise" (Luke 23:43). Let us note that the encounter of Jesus with the thief would happen that same day.

It is interesting that Jesus uses a different word to indicate the place where that repented thief would go: paradise, from gr. paradeisos. It is a word of Persian origin which originally meant a protected park with a fence, a land intended for recreation and pleasure, or a place of bliss and good fortune outside this world.

Jesus told the thief, "Today you will be with me in paradise". On one hand, in the parable of the rich man and Lazarus, Jesus spoke of the "Bosom of Abraham" where the beggar went, and on the other, He spoke of a paradise in which He would be meeting with the thief later. With this, an important question arises, "Are these two places the same place or two distinct places?" Not to deviate from the topic, we will say that Abraham's Bosom is the term coined by the Old Testament to explain the place where the souls of the righteous went. However, after the resurrection of Christ, this same place was elevated to a new dimension and given a new name: paradise. (Read Ephesians 4:8-9 and footnote).[37]

Returning to the topic on hand, the Apostle Paul also teaches about this paradise and says, "I knew a man in Christ above fourteen years ago, (whether in the body, I cannot tell; or whether out of the body, I cannot tell: God knoweth;) such an one caught up to the third heaven. And I knew such a man, (whether in the body, or out of the body, I cannot tell: God knoweth;) How that he was caught up into paradise, and heard unspeakable words, which it is not lawful for a man to utter" (2 Corinthians 12.2-4).

Note here that the Apostle uses two words that are: third heaven and paradise to signal the same place. Then we conclude that, in fact, there is a place of comfort and rest for the souls who served God and a place of torment for those who did not. The Lord Jesus uses this same phrase of paradise when he says, "To him that overcometh will I give to eat of the tree of life, which is in the midst of the paradise of God" (Revelation 2:7).

It is necessary to establish at this point that the aforementioned is neither referring to the lake of fire as explained above, nor to the final destination

---

[37] As for hell, we must not confuse it with the lake of fire (Revelation 19.20; 20.10; 20.14; 20. 15) for this is the final and eternal punishment where the beast (antichrist), the false prophet, death, and even Hades itself are to be cast by God to be punished eternally.

of the saints, who are to live with Christ in the New Jerusalem, according to Revelation 21:1–2. Hell and paradise are temporary places where the sinners and the righteous, respectively, who die must await the final judgment of all souls; and in the case of Christians, the rapture of the Church as we are to see below.

We conclude this point by affirming that we need the salvation so we can go to the place of rest with our Lord Jesus Christ and not be lost in hell.

The Doctrine of Salvation

The doctrine of salvation is based on God's great love for saving mankind from eternal punishment and death. The Bible tells us that Jesus Christ is the means to attain salvation. In the Bible we find that God had to leave His throne of glory and become like us, pay the price for our sins, and die nailed to the cross. Several scriptural passages raise the topic of the salvation that Christ came to bring to mankind.

- "For the Son of man is come to save that which was lost" (Matthew 18:11).
- "And if any man hear my words, and believe not, I judge him not: for I came not to judge the world, but to save the world" (John 12:47).
- "And Jesus said unto him, This day is salvation come to this house, forasmuch as he also is a son of Abraham. For the Son of man is come to seek and to save that which was lost" (Luke 19:9–10).

The doctrine of salvation is a topic that requires an in-depth study and analysis, as it contains many areas that must be considered when addressing the subject, however, because of space and the purpose of this book we'll only discuss this matter shortly.

The Basis of Salvation

If salvation is as important as has been said, then the question that arises in this regard is: "What must we do to be saved?" This was asked by the Philippian jailer to the Apostle Paul in Acts 16 when Paul and Silas were imprisoned. After worshiping God by signing and praising, God shook the Earth and all jail cells were opened. Thinking that every prisoner under his watch had escaped, the jailer was about to take his own life. Before he could, Paul assured him no one had escaped and everyone was still there. Acts 16:30-31 gives an account of what happened next: "And (the jailer) brought them out, and said, Sirs, what must I do to be saved? And they said, Believe on the Lord Jesus Christ, and thou shalt be saved, and thy house."

This question has shaken most people who have heard the message of the gospel and who have understood the need for salvation. What must they do to be saved?

The Plan of Salvation

God has established a plan through which everyone can attain salvation and is freed from eternal damnation. Although such a plan may vary according to religious tradition, most of the Christian world agrees on five fundamental steps taken from the Bible by which human beings can attain the salvation of their souls.

Step one. You must recognize that you are a sinner.

The first part in the process of salvation is to accept and recognize that one is a sinner. From the moment mankind fell in Eden (as we said in the previous chapters), the whole human race also fell and therefore we are sinners. The Bible says, "For all have sinned, and come short of the glory of God" (Romans 3:23).

The entire human race has sinned and needs to be redeemed by Jesus Christ.

> As it is written, There is none righteous, no, not one: There is none
> that understandeth, there is none that seeketh after God. They
> are all gone out of the way, they are together become unprofitable;
> there is none that doeth good, no, not one. Romans 3:10–12

It must be recognized that because of the original sin (The sin of Adam and Eve), everyone is now considered a sinner.

Step two. You must accept Jesus Christ as your personal savior.

The second part in the process of salvation is to accept that there is only one who could pay the price for our souls: Jesus Christ, who gave His life for us.

> This is a faithful saying, and worthy of all acceptation,
> that Christ Jesus came into the world to save sinners;
> of whom I am chief. 1 Timothy 1:15

Jesus came into the world to save sinners and in His name, we have salvation just as the scripture says in Acts 4:11-12, "Neither is there salvation in any other: for there is none other name under heaven given among men, whereby we must be saved."

However, anyone who wants to be saved must unfailingly accept Jesus Christ in their heart, and they must follow Him and serve Him. John explains it saying, "He came unto his own, and his own received him not. But as many as received him, to them gave he power to become the sons of God, even to them that believe on his name" (John 1:11–12).

Jesus Christ came to conquer hearts, but we must accept Him in our hearts willingly, for He is the only one who can save us.

Step three. You must repent with all your heart.

The third part in the process of salvation is repentance. This was precisely the center of Jesus Christ's preaching as well as the Apostles' preaching. For example, Peter told his listeners: "Repent, and be baptized every one of you in the name of Jesus Christ for the remission of sins, and ye shall receive the gift of the Holy Ghost" (Acts 2:38)

If we can observe in this part of Peter's preaching, repentance is put before baptism and clarifies the purpose of baptism: for the forgiveness of sins.

The other point to consider about repentance is the relationship it has with death. The Bible says that the wage of sin is death (Romans 6:23). In other words, human beings must die for committing sins, but God has given us the chance to avoid death through repentance and baptism, interpreted as dying to sin and being born again, respectively.

Repentance is then a fundamental requirement because it means that the believer dies to his sins and to his sinful ways, and lives for Christ.

Step four. You must be baptized.

The fourth part in the process of salvation is the subject of entry or new birth, as mentioned in the previous point. No one can enter the kingdom of God and Christ without first passing through the door of entry. This door is baptism or better known as the new birth. Although we will be discussing this point later, it is sufficient for now to mention that baptism is a requirement for salvation.

Jesus established the requirement of baptism for all who want to enter heaven. We see this when He said to Nicodemus, "Verily, verily, I say unto thee, Except a man be born again, he cannot see the kingdom of God" (John 3:3). He also established it for all people without exception stating, "He that believeth and is baptized shall be saved; but he that believeth not shall be damned" (Mark 16:16).

Step five. You must live a life of holiness.

Finally, anyone who wants to be saved must unfailingly live in holiness. The Bible says, "Follow peace with all men, and holiness, without which no man shall see the Lord" (Hebrews 12:14).

The word holiness means set aside from bad things to serve God. God claims a holy place far from the world and its pleasures. True Christianity is lived in holiness, for we are light in this world. Although this point will be explored later, for now we will only say that a non-holy life can rob the Christian of salvation.

Conclusion

We conclude this chapter by emphasizing the need to understand that God has done a great work by redeeming us from our sins and giving us the greatest gift, the salvation of our souls. That is why as children of God we must always take care of it with fear and trembling, but above all with a lot of love, because the price was very high.

Chapter 10

Repentance

≈

Repent ye therefore, and be converted, that your sins may be blotted out,
when the times of refreshing shall come from the presence of the Lord.

ACTS 3:19

Repentance is a subject that is often set aside when talking about Christian life. However, it is one of the core topics in the process of conversion of a Christian. It is true that there are many churches that may not pay attention to it, however, it must be taught as part of the Christian doctrine. It is for this reason that in this chapter we will be talking about the importance, meaning and impact of repentance on the lives of believers.

Definition

In our common language, repentance means: regret or pain for having done something wrong. However, the Greek translation for repentance is metanoia and means: "A total change in attitude and way of thinking and acting". Repentance means a change of mind. Grudem broadens it as follows, "Repentance is a heartfelt sadness due to sin, a renunciation of sin, and a sincere purpose to forget it and walk in obedience to Christ."[38]

---

[38] Wayne A. Grudem. *Cómo entender la salvación: Una de las siete partes de la Teología Sistemática de Grudem.* (Nashville, TN: Editorial Zondervan, 2013) Pg. 172.

The Importance of Repentance

Repentance is the key to a successful conversion to Christianity which is linked to baptism and new birth and must be given great importance in the Christian life. We must consider that no one should be baptized without first making sure that they have had true repentance.

The Teaching of Repentance

Repentance was strongly preached and demanded by our Lord Jesus Christ. Basically, it was one of the topics He talked about most. The typical phrase of Jesus was, "Repent ye: for the kingdom of heaven is at hand" (Matthew 3:2, Matthew 4:17, and Mark 1:15).

Jesus went from village to village announcing the good news of the kingdom and promoting a radical change in lives of people. Not only did Christ preach repentance, but the apostles also took on this practice. They taught and preached about it to all those who wished to seek the Lord: "Repent ye therefore, and be converted, that your sins may be blotted out, when the times of refreshing shall come from the presence of the Lord" (Acts 3:19).

It Is One of the Elements for Change

Another thing to consider when we talk about repentance is that this is an indispensable component for the change of a person. In other words, there can be no real change in a person if he/she does not experience true repentance.

One of the most notorious cases instances which showcases an instant repentance was witnessed in Zacchaeus. This man, who was a tax collector, lived a life which was not very pleasant in the eyes of the Jews and therefore before God, had a personal encounter with Christ. Zacchaeus had the privilege of welcoming the Master into his home and hearing His words. After the encounter with Jesus, Zacchaeus made a radical change and recognized that he had let many down and a compassion for the poor grew in him. This radical change made Christ very happy, and consequently said, "Today salvation has come to this house" (read the whole story, Luke 19:1–10).

We can learn from Zacchaeus's case that preaching the gospel should encourage people to review their actions and make a resolution to fix those things that are not being done according to God's will, and thereby decide to change. Zacchaeus, hearing Jesus, realized that he had robbed many by demanding amounts of money from them that the Roman Empire was not asking for, but his heart also aligned with Christ's mission, which is to help the poor and most unfortunate. This is true repentance.

It Is One of God's Demands

Repentance became a demand from God for all those who wished to seek Him or for those who received an opportunity to change. We have an example of this in John 8 where the Bible gives an account of a sinful woman who was about to be stoned because she was found in adultery. She is brought before the Lord, but instead of condemning her, Jesus confronts her accusers insisting that whoever is free from sin to cast the first stone. Then, upon justifying her, Jesus told her, "Go, and sin no more" (John 8:11).

God demanded repentance from the religious leaders as well, so that they would not put religion above mercy. The Pharisees and religious leaders had forgotten those who needed God, so Christ strongly rebuked them. "But go ye and learn what that meaneth, I will have mercy, and not sacrifice: for I am not come to call the righteous, but sinners to repentance" (Mat. 9:13).

The Elements of Repentance

As we closely study repentance, we discover that there are certain components that make it possible for repentance to take place and consequently that there is specific process so that it is done correctly. This process includes: the understanding of sin, the feeling of having failed God, and the proper action of change.

Understanding Sin

For repentance to be done effectively, one of the first things the sinner must do is recognize their sin. If this doesn't occur, nothing is going to happen in the individual's life. That is, if there is no awareness of sin, then the individual would not know what they need to repent from. The sinner must know that he has offended God and that without God's forgiveness, he is totally lost.

Understanding sin implies a recognition of how horrendous the sinful act is in the eyes of God, for He is holy and cannot accept sin.

One of the examples that comes to mind is when the Apostle Peter witnessed the miraculous fishing and afterwards said, "Depart from me; for I am a sinful man, O Lord" (See Luke 5:1–8). Although this has no relation to what we are talking about, we can see that Peter could recognize how holy Jesus was and how sinful he was. This is exactly what true repentance does, it makes you realize that you are a sinner and in need of Christ.

The Feeling of Having Sinned

The second component in repentance is regarding the feeling that is created by having sinned. That is, when a person is aware that God is holy and they are very sinful, a feeling of pain and sorrow is created because they recognize that they have failed God. (Read 2 Corinthians 7:9–10.) The feeling of having failed God is manifested in two ways.

First, there is sadness because you have sinned. A repented person recognizes the sadness in his heart is because of having committed so much sin or for having failed God.

This is precisely what Peter experienced by having failed Christ when he denied Him three times. The Bible says that when the rooster crowed as the Lord had told him, Peter wept bitterly (Matthew 26:75). Although it can seem contrary because joy is found in Jesus, but this feeling is one of the greatest signs to know that you are truly sorry, as it gives you a deep sadness for offending God. Incidentally, if someone sins and feels nothing, he must stop and reconsider, as it is very likely that he did not recognize that he has failed God, or he simply does not care anymore.

The second feeling that is created in genuine repentance is to feel unworthy before God. When one begins to hear the word of God and lets the word of God do its intended job, it is very common to feel guilty and hurt for having offended God; but perhaps the strongest feeling is to feel unworthy of Him. This feeling of indignation is precisely what Peter felt, as we said above, when he said to Jesus, "Depart from me; for I am a sinful man, O Lord" (Luke 5:8). Here, albeit in a different context, Peter felt unworthy to stand before someone as holy and as powerful as our Lord Jesus.

Repenting of Your Own Free Will

Finally, true repentance must come of the individual's own free will and not through coercion. This implies that the sinner feels the weight of his guilt and personally decides to do something to remedy that guilt, so he chooses to make a change in his life and fix it or get right with God.

The truly repented person does not wait for their sin to be discovered before repenting, but recognizes that the sin itself is abhorrent, to the point that they just confess the sin and walks away. On the other hand, nobody can, or should, force a person to repent, because in that case it will not be a genuine repentance. This happens many times with parents who force their children into taking that step and repenting. Parents force their children and they do it, but these same children only acted by force and not by self-will. Unfortunately, the results of this action are absolutely negative because over time, they abandon their decision, and it is revealed that there never really was a change.

The Three Steps of True Repentance

It is important to note that true repentance has direct effects on the behavior of the individual. In other words, the repented person takes direct action in adjusting his attitude and behavior and makes a radical change, which usually happens instantly.

There are at least three well-marked steps in the life of a person who has experienced genuine repentance, and these are: the confession of sin, the abandonment of sin, and the return to God.

1.   Repentance Leads to Confession of Sins

The first thing a repented person does is, confess their sin. Regardless of how small or large the sin is, or how dirty or low the person has fallen, they recognize that they failed and confess their faults. This is the greatest sign of a repented heart. The person comes before God and/or his authorities, confesses their faults, and is ready to receive the discipline necessary to make amends for the mistake. The opposite of this action is that of an unrepented heart, which usually tends to cover up or hide sin. Believing that we can deceive God is equivalent to deceiving ourselves. (Read Joshua 7 and Proverbs 28:13). Moreover, when there is confession, there is health and forgiveness. (Read Psalms 32:5 and 1 John 1:9). Finally, trying to hide sin, has no benefit, but on the contrary, the person sinks and corrupts more.

2.   Repentance Leads to Abandoning Sin

The second step taken by a repented sinner is to completely abandon sin. When there is true repentance, the desire to sin is broken. In other words, the person has no desire to keep sinning. It doesn't matter if opportunities to sin are presented, the person feels a rejection to sin and voluntarily turns his back on it. It is also important to emphasize that when there is repentance, there is a desire to seek God, and the person usually tries to refrain from all evil. See the example of the prodigal son in Luke 15:11–21.

3.   Repentance Leads to Turning to God

Finally, true repentance leads the person to return to God and seek Him. At the beginning of this chapter it was mentioned that repentance is a change of mind and attitude. The first thing a repented person does is abandon sin and turn to God. The Apostle Peter explains it as follows, "For ye were as sheep going astray; but are now returned unto the Shepherd and Bishop of your souls" (1 Peter 2:25).

A repentant person will try to seek God and abandon the sinful life. The prophet Isaiah, moved by God, speaks to the people of Israel to do just that, to seek Him, and to forsake sin.

> Seek ye the Lord while he may be found, call ye upon him
> while he is near: Let the wicked forsake his way, and the
> unrighteous man his thoughts: and let him return unto
> the Lord, and he will have mercy upon him; and to our
> God, for he will abundantly pardon. Isaiah 55:6–7

One of the fundamental steps for a person to really have a real change in his life is that when he gives himself to Christ, he must have true repentance. If there is repentance, then there will be a change.

Conclusion

We conclude this chapter by emphasizing that anyone who wants to serve God with a sincere heart must seek genuine and true repentance. As we have seen, only a repented person will abandon sin and seek God with all his heart. Therefore, it is recommended for all who work with new people who are coming to Christ, to steer them towards a serious repentance of their sins. That will be the key to real change.

Chapter 11

Baptism

≈

Go ye therefore, and teach all nations, baptizing them in the
name of the Father, and of the Son, and of the Holy Ghost.

MATTHEW 28:19

Baptism is a fundamental element of Christian doctrine which is part
of the process of salvation and serves as the gateway to the kingdom of
heaven. Baptism has been used over the centuries by the Christian church
as a sacred symbol. It also serves to establish a commitment between the
Christian and the Lord Jesus Christ. In this chapter we will learn some
of the most important details concerning baptism, such as its definition
and meaning, and other fundamental teachings such as its institution,
importance, traditional practices, and how the church should administer it.

Definitions

To fully understand the topic at hand, we must start with its definitions,
use, and applications. The dictionary of the royal Spanish academy
defines the word baptism as, "The sacraments of many Christian
Churches, which rare administered by pouring water on the head or
by immersion, and which prints the character of a Christian to those
who receive it". In addition, it adds that in various religions it is used
as "a rite of purification by water".[39] As we can see in this definition,

---

[39] Real academia española, bajo "bautismo". (Royal Spanish academy, under
baptism). ttps://dle.rae.es/?id=5EgBDLb, retrieved 13 June 2019.

there are significant elements concerning the meaning of this word. The dictionary calls it "a sacrament", in addition, it is administered "using water" and as "a rite of purification". We will expand on these words later for they are fundamental to understanding baptism.

Vine, the etymological dictionary of Old and New Testament words, translates the word baptism from the original Greek verb "baptizo," which means, "to dive, to plunge, to immerse". This Greek verb was used to describe the action of introducing fabrics into containers to dye them.

The dictionary defines it as follows, "Baptism, baptize, primarily a frequent form of bapto, to wet. It was used among the Greeks to dye clothes, to draw water by inserting a vessel into a larger one, etc. Plutarco uses it to draw wine by introducing the glass into the bowl (Alexis, 67) and Plato, metaphorically, as being overwhelmed with questions (Eutidemo, 277 D)". [40]

Therefore, we learn that baptism means literally submerging a person in water. Although we will expand on this later, it is necessary to clarify that the Christian church performed baptisms in this way.

Holman's illustrated biblical dictionary says: The word "baptize" is itself an adopted term from the Greek word "baptizo" and adds, few scholars refute that the meaning of the term is "immerse" and not "pour" or "sprinkle". [41]

The same dictionary adds that baptism is "a Christian rite of passage practiced by almost all who profess the Christian faith." He further emphasizes, "In the New Testament era, people who professed to believe in Christ were submerged in water as a public confession of their faith in Jesus, the Savior." [42]

---

[40] Vine. *Diccionario Expositivo de Palabras del Antiguo y Nuevo Testamento exhaustive,* (Kindle Locations 25470-25473). Grupo Nelson. Kindle Edition.

[41] *Diccionario Bíblico Ilustrado: Spanish Edition,* (Kindle Locations 7287-7289). B&H Publishing Group. Kindle Edition.

[42] Ibid (Kindle Locations 7260-7263).

In this last definition, we can note that not only does baptism means "immersion" but it is "a rite of passage" to the Christian life.

We conclude, therefore, that baptism is the sacrament that the church uses as a means of purification of the soul and as a rite of initiation to Christianity. In other words, for a person to be washed from his sins (as we will see below) and to enter Christianity, he needs to be baptized. In addition, this baptism must be conducted by submerging the person in water.

Institution of Baptism

As said above, baptism is one of the most important sacraments (sacred things) of the Christian faith, and part of the process of salvation. Baptism is a fundamental doctrine within the Holy Scriptures and is essential for the person to attain eternal life.

Baptism was established and instituted by our Lord Jesus Christ for all His followers and for the church He established. Even though it was already used in John's ministry, for Christ Himself also participated in it (Matthew 3:13), but Jesus also included it as part of His requirements for His followers. When our Lord established Christianity, one of the instructions to His disciples was to baptize all those who would like to join His movement. One of the most used Biblical passages to refer to this command of Jesus is found in Matthew and Mark. "Go ye into all the world and preach the gospel to every creature. He that believeth and is baptized shall be saved; but he that believeth not shall be damned" (Mark 16:15–16), also read the parallel passage of Matthew 28:19.

The first century Christian church fulfilled the commandment the Lord gave them, since it baptized the people that were being added, and was the common practice of the first disciples and of the same early church. An example of this is reflected in Philip's evangelistic activity, "But when they believed Philip preaching the things concerning the kingdom of God, and the name of Jesus Christ, they were baptized, both men and women" (Acts 8:12).

The importance of Baptism

As we said at the beginning of this chapter, baptism has been a very important practice in the Christian church from the beginning and is one of the requirements to be a part of it. However, there are at least two fundamental issues that we must know about.

Baptism is necessary for salvation

The first thing to establish is that baptism is necessary to attain the salvation of our souls. Jesus said it very clearly in Mark 16:16, "He that believeth and is baptized shall be saved; but he that believeth not shall be damned." With this in mind, we need to consider that our Lord is establishing the process and a requirement for salvation. This process focuses on obedience of His word to believe and be baptized. The Apostle Peter also confirms this when he is speaking about salvation in the time of Noah, saying, "The like figure whereunto even baptism doth also now save us" (1 Peter 3:21). It is important to understand that there is a baptism that corresponds to salvation, (and if there is one that corresponds, there will be others who do not correspond), and that this is to save man from hell and doom. In addition, it is necessary to emphasize that baptism is not used to name people, but rather, as a means so a person can achieve salvation.

Baptism is necessary for the forgiveness of sins

The second element to consider is that baptism is the only means given by God for mankind to be forgiven of all his sins, under the present dispensation of grace. This means that before the death of Christ, (under the law of Moses), the remission of sins was made through the sacrifice of the Passover lamb. However, under the ministry of Christ, a new dispensation is established that is based on God's love, grace, and mercy. Christ replaced the Passover lamb, which was sacrificed and by whose blood the people of Israel were forgiven of their sins. As Christ shed his blood, all the sins of those who shelter beneath it are blotted out. Therefore, all the individuals must do is repent, believe in Christ, and be baptized.

Above, in the definitions we mention that baptism served as a rite of purification, and it is precisely this. It is a function that is activated in everyone who obeys Jesus's command to be baptized for the forgiveness of sins. However, when we talk about baptism for forgiveness of sins there are some things we should know.

1.   There is only one baptism that forgives.

According to the sacred scriptures, there is only one baptism that must be administered to candidates for forgiveness of sins. This single baptism, we find quoted by Paul in Ephesians 4:5 where he says, "One Lord, one faith, one baptism," and the Apostle Peter also ratifies it in 1 Peter 3:21, "...baptism doth also now save us."

Therefore, this single baptism must inevitably be the one established by Jesus and His disciples, and the recipients will only be able to receive it once. That is, the baptism of Christ can only be administered once; however, if a person was baptized in an unsealed baptism, then he can be re-baptized. To corroborate this position, we must consider that John's disciples had to be baptized again at the baptism of Jesus (Acts 19:1–5).

2.   Baptism replaces the sacrifice of the lamb.

Baptism is a ceremony that replaces the sacrifice of the Passover lamb who, under the law of Moses was sacrificed for forgiveness of sins. God had commanded Israel to sacrifice a lamb to redeem His people from their sins, for without shedding of blood is no remission (Hebrews 9:22). This is because the wages of sin are death (Romans 6:23), and each sinful individual had to die for his sins, for this word to be fulfilled. It is in this dimension that our Lord Jesus Christ takes the place of the lamb, goes to the cross, and dies instead of us (Matthew 26:28). Therefore, for man to be forgiven of his sins, the Lord has established a simple process that prevents him from going to death as Jesus did and consists of the following: repenting of his sins, believing in Christ Jesus, and being baptized in His name, for, through His blood, our sins are forgiven (1 John 1:7).

3.   Baptism washes away sins.

Baptism has the power to wash away all sins when it is done in faith and believing with all the heart. That is precisely what Ananias asked Saul, "And now why tarriest thou? Arise, and be baptized, and wash away thy sins, calling on the name of the Lord" (Acts 22:16).

However, this practice of washing was nothing new, as washing and purification was a fundamental part of the Hebrew religion. In fact, God commanded Israel to wash and prepare for their encounter with God in Sinai (Exodus 19:10) and there was a rite of purification in these practices (2 Chronicles 30:19; John 2:6). That is why Jesus taught Nicodemus the need to be born again through water (John 3:5). Indisputably, baptism is an element of purification in the Christian faith and an obligatory need if someone wants to receive forgiveness for his sins. For this reason, the Apostle Peter told the early Christians who heard his message and were moved to repentance, asking him, "What shall we do?" And the Apostle does not hesitate in his answer, "Repent, and be baptized every one of you in the name of Jesus Christ for the remission of sins" (Acts 2:38).

4.   Baptism is necessary to enter the kingdom of Heaven.

Finally, baptism is the gateway to the kingdom of Heaven and the entrance to the membership of the Church, as we mentioned before. Baptism served as a rite of passage to Christianity and the Church. This concept is taken from the words of Jesus when He said to Nicodemus, "Verily, verily, I say unto thee, except a man be born of water and of the Spirit, he cannot enter into the kingdom of God" (John 3:5).

It is important to emphasize that no one can even consider themselves a member of the Church without going through the process of baptism. This has been the common practice of Christ's church since He founded his church. Both John's followers, as was Jesus for a time, as well as followers of Christ had to be initiated through baptism. Historian Lyman says baptism was the ritual that was administered so that people could enter the Church.[43]

The Practice of Baptism

As mentioned above, baptism is one of the greatest sacraments that any Church has since it represents the gateway to membership of the same. However, it is appropriate that we explain a little about the practices of the church and its administration to the believers, that is, how is it carried out? To answer that question, we need to consider two fundamental things.

1.   Baptism Must Be by Immersion in Water

Baptism must be by immersion, since that is how it was administered by the early Church and must still be so by the very definition of the word. In addition, baptism by immersion is a type and figure of death, burial, and resurrection of the Lord Jesus Christ (Romans 6:3–4). Just as Christ died and was buried, the repentant sinner dies to the world and must be buried in the waters of baptism, and then be resurrected in a new creature as with Jesus.

In the Bible we have some examples of people who were baptized and there are indications that they were submerged in water. For example, Philip was evangelizing the Ethiopian eunuch and the time came when the latter asked Philip to baptize him, and the sacred text says that they came to certain water, "And he commanded the chariot to stand still: and they went down both into the water, both Philip and the eunuch; and he baptized him. And when they were come up out of the water, the Spirit of the Lord caught away Philip" (Acts 8:38–39).

As we can see in this verse that both descended into the water, the eunuch was baptized, and then they rose from the water. Although the

---

[43]   J. Lyman Hurlbut, *Historia de la Iglesia*, (Miami, FL 1999) 41.

Bible does not say whether it was a river, a lake, the sea, or some pond, the truth is that they reached "a certain water", they descended to it, and the Ethiopian was baptized.

Another very notable example is that of John the Baptist. It is well known to all that John used this method in his recruitment practices. The Bible reads, "And John also was baptizing in Aenon near to Salim, because there was much water there: and they came, and were baptized" (John 3:23).

Listeners who accepted the teachings of this prophet were submerged in the waters. As explained above, the single definition of the word baptism indicates "submersion" therefore, the corresponding baptism must be by immersion.

So biblical baptism is and must be by immersion and not by sprinkling water, or much less just symbolic. It is interesting to mention that the first baptism by sprinkling (spraying), was recorded by the historian Eusebius in 250 A.D.[44], and this was because the person who was baptized was dying. The church gave its approval to be baptized by pouring water on his head, however, the person did not die and then the church retracted and no longer allowed baptism by sprinkling. It was not until the Council of Ravenna in 1311 AD that this baptism was approved.[45] In addition, the historian Lyman emphasized in his history of the church that baptism was by immersion.[46]

Another matter to consider concerning the practice of baptism is that baptism should be administered only to adult people. Children cannot be baptized because there is no awareness of sin in them (James 4:16–17). The baptism of infants has never been the practice of the church of the first centuries. This kind of baptism was approved by the Church at the Council of Ravenna in 1311 AD. However, these baptisms lack biblical support, and were highly criticized even within the prevailing Church.

[44] P. L. Maurer, *Eusebio: Historia de la iglesia,* (Grand Rapids MI, 1999) 240.

[45] https://www.scribd.com/document/79850148/BAUTISMO. Consultado el 24 de Julio, 2019.

[46] J. Lyman Hurlbut, *Historia de la iglesia,* (Miami, FL 1999) 41.

2. Baptism Must Be in the Name of Jesus

The other important aspect of baptism is how it should be administered. How is it done? What is said? Although we recognize that there are differences in the Christian people regarding this, however, we recognize that the baptism that corresponds to salvation must be in the name of Jesus. To better understand this position, let's look at the following explanation of the topic.

The commandment of Jesus. We must begin with Jesus's commandment on baptism. The Lord Jesus Christ told His disciples, "Go ye therefore, and teach all nations, baptizing them in the name of the Father, and of the Son, and of the Holy Ghost" (Matthew 28:19).

If we carefully observe the commandment of Jesus Christ to His disciples in Matthew 28:19, it contains a name. The base text of this writing is written in singular and not in the plural. The text reads, in the name of the Father, and of the Son, and of the Holy Ghost. We must note that Father, Son, and Holy Spirit are not names, but titles or offices of God. Therefore, we must ask ourselves, what name should be mentioned when someone is baptized? Someone can argue that this name may be one of the three mentioned, i.e., "Father, Son, and Holy Spirit," however, we must ask ourselves if this is correct.

The practice of the Church. To answer the question from the previous point we must focus on the practice of the church and the early Christians, including the disciples of the Lord. The Apostle Peter, who had received the keys of the kingdom of God through Christ (Matthew 16:19) did not hesitate when he baptized the first brethren. He said, "Repent, and be baptized every one of you in the name of Jesus Christ for the remission of sins, and ye shall receive the gift of the Holy Ghost" (Acts 2:38).

There, the Apostle clearly uses the name of Jesus Christ so that all who hear his sermon may be baptized. The reason is that Peter knew exactly what name Jesus had commanded to use at baptism. That name was Jesus Christ.

Some argue that Peter was wrong not to use the formula of Matthew 28:19. It is necessary to establish, through the Bible, that the Apostles of the Lord were led by the Holy Spirit, as the Lord Jesus Himself had told them, "The Spirit of truth, is come, he will guide you into all truth" (John 16:13), and, "The Holy Ghost, He shall teach you all things" (John 14:26).

In addition, it is important to emphasize that all baptisms practiced by early Christians were in the name of Jesus or Jesus Christ, and not a single baptism appears using the titles, Father, Son, or Holy Spirit. Next, we'll look at a chart teaching the baptisms practiced and baptized using the name of Jesus Christ:

Table 4		
1.	Jews	Acts 2:38
2	Samaritans	Acts 8:16
3.	Gentiles	Acts 10:48, 15:14
4.	Paul	Acts 9:15, 22:16
5.	Romans	Rom. 6:3
6.	Galatians	Gal. 3:27
7.	Corinthians	1 Cor. 1:13
8.	Colossians	Col. 2:12
9.	Ephesians	Acts 19:1–7, Eph. 1:13
10.	The Church	Acts 2:38; 1 Pet. 3:21, James 2:7

Conclusion

We conclude this chapter by mentioning that baptism is a fundamental part of Christianity and should be carefully administered to people who have repented of their sins, who have accepted Christ, and who willing to follow Him. In addition, baptism must be administered by immersion and in the name of our Lord Jesus Christ. Another thing we have learned in this chapter is that all those who want to serve and follow Christ, it is necessary that they be baptized, because, in this case, baptism serves as a gateway.

Chapter 12

The Baptism of the Holy Spirit

≈

*For John truly baptized with water; but ye shall be
baptized with the Holy Ghost not many days hence.*

Acts 1:5

Just as baptism in water is important, it is also important for Christians
to receive the Holy Ghost. This has been the engine that moves the
Church to do what God desires, and it is also what gives life to a child
of God.

A Christian filled with the Holy Spirit becomes a potential in God's
hand. But what does all this mean? How can you receive that power from
God? In this chapter we will explore details about the greatest gift that
God has given to the human being, only after the gift of salvation. This
gift is to receive the Holy Ghost. In addition, we will learn about who
is the Holy Spirit, how it manifests itself, and how it is received; among
other interesting and necessary points for every believer.

Definition

Before we dive into this wonderful topic, we should define a few words
important to the Christian because there is a tendency to misinterpret
the meaning of what the "Spirit" is and the manifestation of the "Holy
Spirit".

The Meaning of the Word "Spirit"

According to the Vine dictionary, the word "spirit" comes from the words ruakh (Hebrew) and pneuma (Greek). These words are translated to "spirit" and literally mean "wind" or "air in motion". However, in the opinion of specialists, its original meaning is breath, that is, the air put in motion by breathing.[47] An example of the use of this word is precisely when God formed man from the dust of the earth, "And the Lord God formed man of the dust of the ground, and breathed into his nostrils the breath of life; and man became a living soul" (Genesis 2:7). So, this word strictly refers to that part of the human being that is linked to the life of the individual.

The Term "Holy Spirit"

On the other hand, when we talk about the "Holy Spirit", the first thing to consider is that this term refers exclusively to God, since He is the Holy Spirit. However, it is also referring to the name that Christian doctrine assigns to the manifestation of God in the lives of believers. The expression Holy Spirit is typical of the New Testament.

The Greek translation in the Old Testament, known as the Septuagint, was used to translate references to the "Spirit of Jehovah", thus avoiding the use of the God's name. Because the authors of the New Testament used the Septuagint to quote the Old Testament, the term Holy Spirit became the standard New Testament denomination for referring to the Spirit of God. It is rare for the Old Testament to speak of the Spirit of God in personified form; rather it refers to something that God bestows on men, or the power and strength with which God acts. On the other hand, the New Testament observes a clear process of personification. The Christian doctrine establishes a very important place for the Holy Spirit in the life of the child of God. Two very significant points are considered here.

---

[47] *Enciclopedia Electrónica Ilumina*, Vine, Loc. cit.

First, Jesus promised that He would send the Holy Ghost to His followers when He said, "It is expedient for you that I go away: for if I go not away, the Comforter will not come unto you; but if I depart, I will send him unto you" (John 16:7).

In this verse we can see that Jesus needed to leave this world, for the Holy Spirit to come, and the reason was simple; it suited them. What Jesus means is that the Holy Spirit would continue with the work He was doing, including comforting and guiding believers.

Second, the Holy Spirit was active in the early Church and was not merely an allegorical, symbolic, or much less mystical matter. One of the biblical texts that best illustrates this thought is when Paul is called to ministry. The text reads, "As they ministered to the Lord, and fasted, the Holy Ghost said, Separate me Barnabas and Saul for the work whereunto I have called them" (Acts 13:2).

Here it is clear that it was the Holy Spirit who called them, and it was not the other apostles, like Peter or John. It is important to note that at the beginning of the early Church, the Holy Spirit dictated orders of what should be done and was present in the decisions the Church had to make.

The Importance of Receiving the Holy Spirit

The most important thing about this chapter is that, as children of God we must receive the Holy Spirit in our lives. That means that God enters our body and life to live. However, the importance of receiving it is not simply because God wants to live in us, but because of the effects it can have in our lives. Next, let's look at the importance of receiving it.

1.   It is Indispensable to Enter the Kingdom of God

The first aspect we should consider about the importance of receiving the Holy Ghost is it is necessary for "entering the kingdom of God." But what does it mean to enter the kingdom of God? Before answering this question, we must say that this postulation is found in Jesus's meeting with Nicodemus (a chief of the Jews) who came to look for him at night. Jesus tells this man, "Verily, verily, I say unto thee, Except a man be born of water and of the Spirit, he cannot enter into the kingdom of God" (John 3:5). Jesus addresses two essential points about the need for the baptism of the Holy Spirit. The first, one must be born again (water and spirit), and the second, without it, one cannot enter the kingdom of God. We'll discuss both points shortly.

The new birth. Considering the above, we can find that here arises the first need for the Spirit: "It is necessary to be born of the Spirit in order to enter the kingdom of God." The doctrine of the New Birth arises due to the need to restore humans completely to the original state in which God created them and the only way to do so is for human beings to be reborn. However, this birth cannot be achieved as Nicodemus thought by entering the mother's womb and being born again. It refers to a divine act in which God regenerates man to his original state, which is understood as the state before having sinned.

This new birth must be carried out first in water through baptism and second, by receiving the Holy Spirit. Both baptisms are done through faith. Repentance and Christ's sacrifice on the cross of Calvary are sufficient for a person to begin a new life and enter the kingdom of God.

The Kingdom of God. The second element has to do with the question: What does the kingdom of God mean? The Kingdom of God can be understood as God's dominion, but it can also be interpreted as that space or place where Christians will spend eternity in and, therefore, the Spirit is required to enter it and to be able to belong to it. Matthew uses the phrase "the Kingdom of Heaven" to refer to the kingdom of God and following Vine's translation, denotes the sphere of God's government.

The word Basileia indicates sovereignty, royal power, and dominion. This term applies specifically to the kingdom of God and of Christ. However, because the earth is the universal stage of rebellion against

God, the kingdom of God must be understood as the sphere in which the government of God is recognized at any time.[48]

Some have interpreted "Kingdom of God" with "salvation", and although it may apply, they are two different things. The kingdom of God encompasses both life on earth and future life where God is to reign permanently, but salvation is to belong to that group of people who are not to go to eternal punishment and are to be close to God.

2. It is Necessary to Receive Life

The second point to consider is the importance of the Holy Spirit in the spiritual future of believers. For this we must consider the apostle Paul's position on the future of Christians. He says, "But if the Spirit of him that raised up Jesus from the dead dwell in you, he that raised up Christ from the dead shall also quicken your mortal bodies by his Spirit that dwelleth in you" (Romans 8:11).

We can understand that the Apostle speaks of an awakening of the mortal body by the Spirit of God that dwells in us. In other words, it is necessary to have the Spirit to receive life after we have died, that is, for the resurrection. This makes sense, because just as God breathed breath in the first man when he was formed from the earth and lived (Genesis 2:7). In the same way, the Spirit will resurrect the son of God who has been made from the dust of the earth and will lift him up.

3. It is Necessary to be Raised with Christ

The other point to consider is what will happen to Christians when Christ comes for us. The text puts it as follows, "Ye were sealed with that Holy Spirit of promise, Which is the earnest of our inheritance until the redemption of the purchased possession, unto the praise of his glory" (Ephesians 1:13–14).

---

[48] W. E. Vine, Op. cit., 340.

Just as the groom in olden times returned to pick up the piece of cloth or garment with which he had gotten engaged to a maiden for marriage, in the same way, when Christ comes for His Church, the Holy Spirit will be the sign that a person has been marked and pointed out by God to go with Christ. Finally, one of the Apostle Paul's recommendations to the Ephesians was not to make the Spirit sad, for this was God's seal or mark that longed awaited the day of redemption. "And grieve not the holy Spirit of God, whereby ye are sealed unto the day of redemption" (Ephesians 4:30).

4.   It is Essential to Receive Spiritual Power

The other important aspect of receiving the Holy Ghost is directly related to power. It is this power that the Lord's disciples would be receiving soon. At least that is what Christ told them, "But ye shall receive power, after that the Holy Ghost is come upon you: and ye shall be witnesses unto me both in Jerusalem, and in all Judaea, and in Samaria, and unto the uttermost part of the earth" (Acts 1:8).

This was a supernatural power given over the disciples to do the work He was sending them to do, which is why Christ told them to stay in Jerusalem and not leave until they received this power from high up (Luke 24:49). They were going to need it along the way.

There are at least four areas in which the Holy Spirit imparts power to believers.

• First, the power to be taught and remember all things of God.

"But the Comforter, which is the Holy Ghost, whom the Father will send in my name, he shall teach you all things, and bring all things to your remembrance, whatsoever I have said unto you" (John 14:26).

The Christian filled with the Holy Spirit receives a supernatural power that teaches him about situations in which he must act and reminds him of those Biblical passages he read on occasion.

- Second, the power to be guided to all truth.

"Howbeit when he, the Spirit of truth, is come, he will guide you into all truth: for he shall not speak of himself; but whatsoever he shall hear, that shall he speak: and he will shew you things to come" John 16:13.

What a wonderful verse! For no one who has received the Holy Ghost and is sensitive to Him can fail to find the truth. This is what God did with Apollos by revealing the truth to him (Acts 18:24–26).

- Third, the power to receive spiritual wisdom.

"But we speak the wisdom of God" (1 Corinthians 2:1–10). In addition, this was one of the requirements that early deacons should have. "Look ye out among you seven men of honest report, full of the Holy Ghost and wisdom, whom we may appoint over this business" (Acts 6:1–6).

The son of God is and must be wise in all aspects, for it is through the Spirit of the Lord that he receives wisdom. Wisdom, to speak, to counsel, to make decisions, in short, for our whole life. That is why one of the symbols of the Holy Spirit is light.

- Fourth, the power to share the good news effectively.

"When the Comforter is come, even the Spirit of truth, which proceedeth from the Father, he shall testify of me: And ye also shall bear witness, because ye have been with me from the beginning" John 15:26–27.

Listening to someone filled with the anointing of God preaching, pleases and converts to the heart. It is sufficient to read the book of Acts to realize that the disciples of the Lord, once they had received the Holy Spirit, spoke the word of God with newfound boldness (Acts 4:13, 29, 31; 13:46; 14:3; 18:26).

The Manifestation of the Holy Spirit

When we study about the Holy Spirit, it is essential to analyze how it manifests itself in the lives of believers. The reason for the study of this phenomenon has to do with the fact that the form and manner in which the Spirit of God manifests itself in believers is often misunderstood. For this reason, some tend to mock or underestimate how the Spirit shows its influence on the lives of Christians.

Biblical Event

In Acts 2:1–4, 14–16, we find the Biblical account of the descent of the Holy Spirit on the early Christians. One of the verses reads, "And they were all filled with the Holy Ghost, and began to speak with other tongues, as the Spirit gave them utterance" (Acts 2:4).

It was during the feast of Pentecost (a Jewish feast that was celebrated 50 days after the Passover feast (Leviticus 23) that the Holy Spirit descended upon the disciples of Jesus. There, the Holy Spirit was manifested for the first time and in a way that surprised all those who were there, who, when they heard and saw the people, considered them drunk. However, this was already announced by the Old Testament prophets. Let's see what the scripture says about these prophecies.

Prophecies in the Old Testament

God had spoken through Old Testament prophets concerning the coming of the Holy Spirit and His manifestation in believers. Although in those moments for them it was something unknown and they did not even fully understand it, now it had become a reality.

The prophet Isaiah had said that God would speak to his people, "For with stammering lips and another tongue" (Isaiah 28:11). The Apostle Paul mentioned this prophecy in 1 Corinthians 14:21, "Therefore, here we have the first element to consider, and it is the stuttering tongue and the strange tongue." This must be understood as that language that is not clear and is distorted when speaking, in a clear reference to the speaking in tongues by the influence of the Holy Spirit as we will see later.

The other matter that was prophesied was the work of the Spirit in the life of the believer, and it has to do with what God would do in the hearts of believers. God said through the same prophet Isaiah, "For I will pour water upon him that is thirsty, and floods upon the dry ground: I will pour my spirit upon thy seed" (Isaiah 44:3). In this verse, the Spirit would come to bring life to whomever would receive Him.

The prophet Ezekiel adds a little more about the work the Spirit would do in the heart of the receiver. "A new heart also will I give you, and a new spirit will I put within you: and I will take away the stony heart out of your flesh, and I will give you an heart of flesh" (Ezekiel 36:26). It is understood through these verses, said via prophets, that God would do the transformative work in the lives of those who would receive Him.

Finally, God also speaks through the prophet Joel, in one of the clearest prophecies about the characteristics and manifestation of the Spirit in the lives of believers. The prophet said, "And it shall come to pass afterward, that I will pour out my spirit upon all flesh; and your sons and your daughters shall prophesy, your old men shall dream dreams, your young men shall see visions: And also upon the servants and upon the handmaids in those days will I pour out my spirit." (Joel 2:28–29).

This is perhaps one of the clearest passages of the Old Testament concerning how the Spirit must work in the lives of those who would possess it. The recipients (without exceptions) will prophesy, dream dreams, and have visions when the Spirit is poured out upon them.

Prophecies in the New Testament

If the subject of the Holy Ghost was spoken in the Old Testament, it strengthened in the New Testament, where it was also prophesied.

John the Baptist was one of the first to announce the coming of the Holy Spirit upon believers. In his preaching he said, "I indeed baptize you with water unto repentance. but he that cometh after me is mightier than I, whose shoes I am not worthy to bear: he shall baptize you with the Holy Ghost, and with fire" (Matthew 3:11).

Here we notice that John not only announces the descent of the Spirit, but also refers to Jesus Christ as the person who is to baptize believers with the Holy Ghost. Note that John is the first to use the word "baptism in the Holy Spirit".

The Lord Jesus Christ also teaches His followers on the same subject and invites His listeners to believe in Him and those who did would receive the reward of "rivers of life", (John 7:37–39). He also encourages His listeners to ask of the Spirit and says, "If ye then, being evil, know how to give good gifts unto your children: how much more shall your heavenly Father give the Holy Spirit to them that ask him?" (Luke 11:13). Jesus's exhortation to His listeners is clear, that if anyone asks for it, He is willing to give it. In addition, Jesus required his disciples to stay in Jerusalem and not go out to carry out evangelism without first receiving the Holy Spirit.

"Behold, I send the promise of my Father upon you: but tarry ye in the city of Jerusalem, until ye be endued with power from on high" (Luke 24:49). The reason is very simple, they were going to need the help of the Spirit to be able to carry out the work.

As we can see in these prophecies, God promises His people the advent of the Holy Spirit upon all flesh, and Jesus also promises them to His disciples. So these promises of God were fulfilled on the day of Pentecost and from then on, the Church was an active participant in this experience.

Fulfillment of Prophecies

To corroborate the previous point, we should quickly analyze a list of biblical passages in which the prophecies mentioned above, both from the Old and New Testaments, were carried out.

- Acts 2:1–4, The first disciples – "And they were all filled with the Holy Ghost..."
- Acts 4:31, The first congregation – "And they were all filled with the Holy Ghost..."
- Acts 8:17, The brothers in Samaria – "Then laid they their hands on them, and they received the Holy Ghost."
- In Acts 9:17, to Paul – "and be filled with the Holy Ghost..."
- In Acts 10:44, in the house of Cornelius the centurion – "the Holy Ghost fell on all of them which heard the word."

And the list goes on and on...

Demonstration and Evidence of Having Received the Holy Spirit

Another point to mention when studying the reception of the Holy Ghost has to do with the question: "How do we know if someone has received the Holy Ghost?" This is a very important question, as it often creates some confusion as to whether a person has already received the Spirit, when he has not and vice versa. There are people who say they haven't received it, when in fact, they already have it. There are at least three signs to recognize that a person has been filled with the Holy Ghost; we call it "evidence".

The Initial Evidence is to Speak in Other Languages

The first evidence that can be seen in a person who has been filled with the Holy Ghost is to speak in other tongues. Some of the basic passages for this position are found in the book of Acts of the Apostles.

The first incident occurs while the disciples are waiting for the promise of Jesus (Luke 24:49). They were in the upper room (a room on the roof of a house) and there descended the Father's promise. The verse reads, "And suddenly there came a sound from heaven as of a rushing mighty wind … And there appeared unto them cloven tongues like as of fire, and it sat upon each of them. And they were all filled with the Holy Ghost, and began to speak with other tongues, as the Spirit gave them utterance" (Acts 2:1–4).

Just imagine! That day was historic, as much had been said about this and many were expecting it. They received the Holy Ghost and spoke in other languages. This incident marks the great beginning of an escalation of manifestations of the Spirit in the lives of early believers. Therefore, this study is essential – for this was the fulfillment of the promises of the Old Testament and the promises of Jesus.

The second incident occurred in Samaria with Philip. Peter and John had reached Samaria, where there was a group of Christians baptized in water in the name of Jesus, but who had not yet been baptized with the Holy Spirit. For this reason, Peter and John laid their hands on them and they received the Holy Spirit (Acts 8:17).

This is the only passage in Acts where it is not mentioned that believers have spoken in new tongues and it is highly debated. However, many modern Pentecostal groups believe that they did, because Simon the Magician had wanted to buy the gift of the Holy Spirit because he had seen a great wonder, which many theologians suppose, was the gift of tongues manifested in the Samaritans. On the other hand, in Luke's account of the scope of Pentecost the continuity of the Pentecost of Acts 2 is seen.

When the apostles who were in Jerusalem heard that Samaria had received the word of God, they sent Peter and John there; who, after arriving, prayed for them to receive the Holy Spirit, for it had not yet descended on any of them, but they had only been baptized in water in the name of Jesus.

"Then they laid hands on them, and they received the Holy Spirit..." (Acts 8:14–17). If we consider the literary unit of Luke's account, we must presume that when he says they received the Holy Spirit (Acts 2:1–4 and 17; 10:45–46; and 19:1-6) it refers to the same time they spoke in tongues.

The third incident occurred in the house of Cornelius, when he was attentively listening to the word Peter was speaking to him and suddenly the Spirit descended upon all who heard the Apostle. "After having received the visit of God and Peter's instructions, the Holy Ghost fell on all of them which heard the word for they heard them speak with tongues, and magnify God" (Acts 10:44–46). Everyone in that house spoke in tongues. Let us note that Cornelius is the first Gentile to receive the Father's promise.

A fourth event is mentioned in Acts 19 when the Apostle Paul finds disciples of John and asks them if they have received this great gift from God. However, they are surprised by the question and answer that they do not even know if there is a Holy Spirit. After this, they pray for them and what happens next is that "the Holy Ghost came on them; and they spake with tongues and prophesied" (Acts 19:1–6) These disciples, when they received the Holy Spirit, also spoke in tongues.

Therefore, speaking in tongues is then the initial evidence of having received the Holy Spirit, this was precisely what happened with the early Church and the early Christians. Now, it is also worth asking, what is speaking in tongues? Here is a brief explanation.

The practice of speaking in tongues.

As mentioned in the previous paragraph. Speaking in tongues was a common practice of the early Church and of the early Christians. The Apostle Paul tries to explain this topic and writes a whole chapter on this reality concisely to the Church of Corinth (1 Corinthians 14).

Paul begins by talking about the gifts of the Spirit and the importance of prophesying (preaching) in reference to spiritual gifts. Let's see how he develops the theme through the chapter.

- In v. 2 it says, "For he that speaketh in an unknown tongue speaketh not unto men, but unto God. Here the first important point arises." When the believer speaks in tongues, he speaks to God and not to men.
- In v.4 the apostle says, "He that speaketh in an unknown tongue edifieth himself; but he that prophesieth edifieth the church." This is another fundamental point. The believer receives edification when he speaks in tongues. Someone can argue and ask what kind of edification, since they don't understand what the person is saying. This edification is associated with the strength, faith, and blessing that a person receives when God is filling him with His spirit. Let us remember that Christ said that the work of the Spirit was to "comfort the believer" (John 14:26; 15:26; and 16:7).
- In v.22 he also teaches the "why" of speaking in tongues. In verse 21 Paul uses the prophecy of Isaiah 28:11–14 (where the word "stuttering tongue" is used). However, in verse 22 it says, "tongues are for a sign, not to them that believe, but to them that believe not." This may then be the third reason why it is spoken in tongues: this is for testimony to those who are not Christians, or to those who do not believe; as was the case of the Israelites, when Isaiah's prophecy was given.
- Finally, in v.39 Paul closes by advising the church that, although the person who receives the Spirit does not understand what he speaks in tongues, he should not be prevented from speaking. "And forbid not to speak with tongues. But all this must be done decently and in order" (V. 40) and that must be the norm.

Physical Demonstrations

Apart from the earlier biblical passages that prove that believers spoke in other tongues as initial evidence of having received the Holy Ghost, there is also physical evidence. It is interesting to note that others noticed the descent of the Spirit upon them. For example, the first time the Spirit descended in Acts and Peter was explaining the occurrence to surprised listeners. Peter said, "He hath shed forth this, which ye now see and hear" (Acts 2:33). Let us note the words "you see and hear". In other words, whoever receives the Holy Ghost emits voices and actions that are heard and seen. It is normal to observe a person who, when receiving the Holy Spirit, raises their hands and praises God strongly; weeps, not with sadness but with joy; sometimes jumps and leaps with joy; and best of all, speaks in tongues.

The physical demonstration they observed fulfilled Joel's prophecy. "And they were all amazed, and were in doubt, saying one to another, What meaneth this? … But this is that which was spoken by the prophet Joel" (Acts 2:12– 17). Joel had said that those who receive the Spirit will see visions, dream dreams, and even in heaven signs will be seen.

Another incident takes place when they receive the Spirit and begin to speak the word of God freely and easily. "The place was shaken where they were assembled together; and they were all filled with the Holy Ghost, and they spake the word of God with boldness" (Acts 4:31). This sign was one of the most important signs with the early Christians; for everyone who received the Holy Spirit received an ease in speaking the word of God.

One well-known case was that of Simon the Magician. "And when Simon saw that through laying on of the apostles' hands the Holy Ghost was given, he offered them money" (Acts 8:18). He clearly saw that people who received the Spirit experienced certain manifestations in their lives. This caught the attention of the magician and asked to receive what they had received.

Then we must establish that those who received the Holy Ghost showed certain physical signs in their bodies that demonstrated that something supernatural was going on in them. Those around them saw and heard something very tremendous that left them stunned and perplexed.

Demonstrations of Power

Perhaps one of the important parts of receiving the Holy Ghost is the fulfillment of Jesus's words to His disciples, when He said to them, "But ye shall receive power, after that the Holy Ghost is come upon you" (Acts 1:8).

Power is the greatest demonstration that a person has received God's greatest gift (after salvation). A person receives a spiritual strength to do many things he could not do before.

Let's look at some examples of this power.

The first miracle operated by the apostles under the influence of the Holy Ghost was the healing of a lame man from birth (Acts 3:1–10). This time Peter speaks to the lame saying, "Silver and gold have I none; but such as I have give I thee: In the name of Jesus Christ of Nazareth rise up and walk" (Acts 3:6).

From then on there would come many more miracles, to such an extent that the writer of the book of Acts says, "And by the hands of the apostles were many signs and wonders wrought among the people" (Acts 5:12).

Another demonstration of this power is manifested in the characteristics of the believer, as we observe in Stephen. "And Stephen, full of faith and power, did great wonders and miracles among the people" (Acts 6:8).

Personal Transformation

Finally, the other evidence of having received the Holy Spirit is the change in the person's life and the manifestation of the fruits of the Spirit (Galatians 5:22–23). For many, this last point may not be as important, because usually, more attention is given to the works of miracles and other aspects that cause sensation. However, change and personal transformation is the greatest work of the Holy Ghost in a person.

How to Receive the Holy Ghost

Let's close this chapter with some tips for receiving the Holy Ghost, as sometimes there are people who wonder how they can receive it.

Receiving the Holy Spirit

Sometimes it becomes a little complicated for people to receive the Holy Ghost, especially for those who are quiet and reserved. In those cases, someone may come to the way of thinking that "that's not for me." However, the Bible also records a case in which those who had already been baptized had not yet been able to receive it. This happened in Samaria during the evangelistic preaching that was taking place. The people were being baptized by the movement that was being carried out, however it was not until Peter and John came to oversee the work. They prayed for them to receive it, which happened when they laid their hands on them (Acts 8:14–17).

This incident makes it clear that not all cases are like that of Cornelius who with just listening to the word of God, was already speaking in tongues (Acts 10:48), but that there will be those who would struggle a little to receive it; but that is something to look for.

How do I receive the Holy Ghost?

I believe that to receive the Holy Spirit there is no "magic" formula or some trick or much less someone taking classes to receive this gift that God has already given by faith to believers. What we do believe is that there are certain requirements that are necessary for a person to receive it more easily as we expos it next.

1. You must WANT to receive it. The first requirement to receive the Holy Ghost is to want it. By simple logic, God will not give the gift of the Spirit to one who does not wish to receive it. At least that's what Christ told all His listeners. "In the last day,

that great day of the feast, Jesus stood and cried, saying, If any man thirst, let him come unto me, and drink. He that believeth on me, as the scripture hath said, out of his belly shall flow rivers of living water. (But this spake he of the Spirit, which they that believe on him should receive" (John 7:37–39). In this passage we can clearly see that only those who thirst for the Spirit can receive it. All you must do is get close to get a drink of it.

2. You must ASK for it. The second requirement is that the interested person must ask for it. There are many occasions when we are encouraged to ask God what we desire and one of the key verses for this desire is the following said by the Lord. "If ye then, being evil, know how to give good gifts unto your children: how much more shall your heavenly Father give the Holy Spirit to them that ask him?" (Luke 11:13).

3. You should SEEK it until you receive it. The third requirement is to search for Him. When we speak of seeking Him, it is not that God has been lost and not found, but that we must pray, and pray until we receive it. That was precisely the commandment of Jesus. "And, behold, I send the promise of my Father upon you: but tarry ye in the city of Jerusalem, until ye be endued with power from on high" (Luke 24:49). They spent ten days waiting for Christ's promise, in prayer and supplication, but on the tenth day the Lord blessed them with this special gift. God will always give His children His blessing when they seek Him wholeheartedly.

4. You PRAY for the Holy Spirit. Finally, and only in the last instance, a special prayer must be made for the one who wants to receive it. This is what Peter and John did with the Samaritans, since they had gone through the process of conversion, heard the word, and been baptized, but had not yet received the baptism of the Holy Spirit. "Then laid they their hands on them, and they received the Holy Ghost" (Acts 8:17). Sometimes it takes a little more pressure for that power to descend over the believers. This is the touch of those who have been anointed and selected by God as ministers, to pray for brothers and sisters by laying their hands on them. Sometimes there are those who have God's gift of being able to pray for people and they receive the gift of the Holy Ghost.

Conclusion

As we have seen in this chapter, we have learned many things about one of the greatest gifts the believer has received, and this is the fullness of the Holy Ghost. In addition, we have learned the impact on the lives of believers to be filled with this wonderful power that Christ left us to serve Him. Therefore, it must be searched and sought after until it is received, because it is a great necessity for the Christian journey.

Chapter 13

Holiness

≈

Because it is written: Be ye holy; for I am holy.

1 PETER 1:16

One of the practices that distinguishes the true Christian from religious and false Christians is the life of holiness that those who serve God lead. Holiness is what distinguishes a liberal church from a conservative one. It is a very important and necessary topic, especially in a time as dangerous as today. When we talk about being conservative, we are not talking about being legalistic or extremist, but one who departs from this sinful world. We know that God is holy, but can mortals be holy? In this chapter we will explore all the ins and outs of what a holy life is and how to live a holy life before God.

Definition

The word holy and its various applications come from the Greek word jagios, which means "separated for God", and in its moral and spiritual sense, "separated from sin and consecrated to God". It applies to both God and His people. This word also has a strict relationship with the condition of those who are set apart for God. This word is rooted in the

Hebrew text Qadsh, which has a strict religious sense and applies to both objects, places, and days.[49]

An application of this word is seen when God tells His people, "And ye shall be unto me a kingdom of priests, and an holy nation" (Exodus 19:6). In addition, it is used when referring to water in the purification process in ceremonies of Hebrew worship, "And the priest shall take holy water in an earthen vessel" (Numbers 5:17). Finally, it refers to the Sabbath that the children of Israel should keep throughout their generations, "Ye shall keep the sabbath; therefore, for it is holy unto you: every one that defileth it shall surely be put to death" (Exodus 31:14).

As we can see, God had sanctified everything that had a relationship or was in connection with Him or His service, in such a way that water, utensils, people, and even the day that had been dedicated were considered holy.

In our context, "a holy person" is a Christian person separated from the world to serve God, as some biblical texts say. (Exodus 19:6 and 22:31; Deuteronomy 33:3 and 8; Psalm 50:5 and 106:16; Daniel 7:21; and Acts 9:13, 32 and 41.) This matter of holiness has a strict relationship with our Lord because it speaks of the nature of God and how He wants people to understand it. In other words, holiness speaks of God, His character, and His nature. God is holy morally (Leviticus 11:44) and in power (1 Samuel 6:20). He is the Holy One of Israel (Isaiah 1:4), He is called the Holy God (Isaiah 5:16) and the Holy One (Isaiah 40:25). His name is Holy, "For thus saith the high and lofty One that inhabiteth eternity, whose name is Holy" (Isaiah 57:15).

In other words, everything that refers to God, His presence, His space, His works, and His field of action is holy. Just look at the words He said to Moses when he appeared to him in a burning bush, "Draw not nigh

---

[49] W.E. Vine, Diccionario expositivo de palabras del Antiguo y Nuevo Testamento, (Expository Dictionary of Old and New Testament Words) (Nashville, TN: Grupo Nelson, 2007).

hither: put off thy shoes from off thy feet, for the place whereon thou standest is holy ground" (Exodus 3:5).

So, taking into consideration the paragraph above, not only is God holy, but everything that comes close to Him must be sanctified. Therefore, we as Christians must be holy too. The Apostle Paul uses the word "holy" many times when referring to Christians. (See: Romans 8:27, 1 Corinthians 14:33, Ephesians 1:1, Philippians 1:1, Colossians 1:1.)

The Need for Holiness

Holiness is a fundamental aspect in Christianity and should not be an isolated or a neglected matter, but something important and necessary for the child of God. In this section we will study the reason for this need and the repercussions of departing from it.

Holiness is Necessary for Salvation

First, we need to understand that holiness has a direct relationship with the salvation of the individual. This is perhaps one of the greatest needs a Christian has concerning his salvation. The Bible says, "For we shall see Him (God) as He is. And every man that hath this hope in him purifieth himself, even as he is pure" (1 John 3:2–3).

As we can see here, our God has made things very clear. If anyone wants to see Him one day, then he must be sanctified. Another widely known verses also used by the proponents of this position is found in Hebrews. It says: Follow peace with all men, and holiness, without which no man shall see the Lord" (Hebrews 12:14).

In this last verse, it is confirmed again that no one can see God face to face, unless that person is sanctified. It is important to consider that if God demanded His people to sanctify the water, the utensils, the days, the priests who officiated the services, and even the people of Israel, He also expects this from His church – which was washed with his precious blood.

Holiness as a Requirement to Serve God

The second point to consider concerning holiness is pertaining to serving God. Although God wants every person to serve Him and give themselves to Him, nevertheless, God demands a holy life from all those who wish to serve Him. When we study this topic in the scriptures, we can find that God was very direct with those He called to serve Him. For example, to the priests of the Old Testament, God said, "But he shall not defile himself, being a chief man among his people, to profane himself. They shall not make baldness upon their head, neither shall they shave off the corner of their beard, nor make any cuttings in their flesh" (Leviticus 21:4–7).

Therefore, priests were consecrated to God and should be careful in many areas of their lives. Some may think that if a person was not a priest, then they were exempt; however, God's people in general should be holy. We observed this when God was going down to Sinai to give them the laws. God commanded all people to sanctify themselves. "Go unto the people, and sanctify them today and tomorrow, and let them wash their clothes, And be ready against the third day: for the third day the Lord will come down in the sight of all the people upon mount Sinai" (Exodus 19:10–11).

As for the Church, we must say that the same words and commandments on holiness also apply, especially since today's church is that sacred place of God, royal priesthood, and holy nation (1 Peter 2:9). Moreover, the Apostle Paul teaches us that we were chosen by God before the foundation of the world, precisely to be holy. "According as he hath chosen us in him before the foundation of the world, that we should be holy and without blame before him" (Ephesians 1:4). We have been called to serve Him and for that we must be sanctified.

Holiness as a Lifestyle

Holiness in the church is not a purely symbolic or simply spiritual matter. True holiness is something that is practiced in daily life. That is, our behavior shows that we live a holy life. Holiness includes all our Christian life, at all times and in all places. It applies not only to the outer man but also to the inner man, who in perfect harmony yield to God's will. One of the clearest passages concerning this was preached by the Apostle Peter. "As he which hath called you is holy, so be ye holy in all manner of conversation; Because it is written, Be ye holy; for I am holy" (1 Peter 1:15–16).

As we can see, this verse reiterates all that we have said earlier. He who called us is holy, so we must be holy too, and that manifests itself in the way we live our lives.

Paul also exhorts the Corinthians to remain clean in their entirety. "Having therefore these promises, dearly beloved, let us cleanse ourselves from all filthiness of the flesh and spirit, perfecting holiness in the fear of God" (2 Corinthians 7:1).

The Apostle is quite clear in specifying the meaning of holiness by emphasizing that it has to do with cleansing oneself from all contamination of the flesh and spirit. The flesh here refers to our body and the spirit refers to our interior.

It is important to mention that if holiness that does not affect our way of life, it is simply a religious fantasy. God wants us to show men that we are different people, and the only way to show it is with our behavior.

Inner Holiness

True holiness begins within the human being and then manifests itself externally. This is precisely where the holiness of the person is looked at, for all behavior comes from the heart. The Lord Jesus Christ made it very clear, "For out of the heart proceed evil thoughts, murders, adulteries, fornications, thefts, false witness, blasphemies" (Matthew 15:19).

Inner holiness deals with the purity of our thoughts, feelings, and all those desires that only we know. This was the problem that the religious people of the time of Jesus had and which our Master had to reprimand harshly. "Woe unto you, scribes and Pharisees, hypocrites! for ye make clean the outside of the cup and of the platter, but within they are full of extortion and excess. Thou blind Pharisee, cleanse first that which is within the cup and platter, that the outside of them may be clean also" (Matthew 23:25–26). For these religious people, holiness consisted of showing men as isolated, select and very holy people, but the truth is that they were failing from within, since they had evil in their hearts.

Living Holiness from Within

Anyone who wants to please the Lord must live a holy life which must begin from within. That is, they must have good feelings, good thoughts, and above all they must take care of what comes out as well.

1.   The Holiness of the Mind

The first area in which we must work is in our minds. The mind is the engine that drives everything that we think. With our minds we process all kinds of thoughts, both clean and sinful. Therefore, holiness begins by replacing all dirty, evil, and negative thoughts with pure, holy, and good thoughts. The Bible advises us that we must take captive every thought to the obedience of Christ (2 Corinthians 10:5) and advises us to filter out every thought that comes to our minds and think only. "Whatsoever things are true, whatsoever things are honest, whatsoever things are just, whatsoever things are pure, whatsoever things are lovely, whatsoever things are of good report; if there be any virtue, and if there be any praise, think on these things" (Philippians 4:8).

2.   The Holiness of the Heart

The other area in which holiness must be manifested has to do with the heart. The heart is the seat of our emotions and our desires. It is in the heart where our purest and lowest feelings are born. An unsanctified heart can give birth to what Jesus says in Matthew 15:19, "For out of the heart proceed evil thoughts, murders, adulteries, fornications, thefts, false witness, blasphemies."

Moreover, it is in the heart that all sinful feelings such as hatred, spite, bitterness, deception, pride, and envy are created. The true Christian has submitted his/her mind and heart to Christ and has been crucified together with Him. Anything mentioned above should not manifest itself in a person who has already been washed and forgiven.

3. The Sanctity of our Words

Our tongue has a direct connection with our minds and with our hearts, for we use it to express what we feel and what we think. That is why it is a very important subject when talking about holiness. Jesus said, "For out of the abundance of the heart the mouth speaketh" (Matthew 12:34). We need to pay attention to the use of the tongue.

James is the biblical writer who gives us a dissertation on this small part of the body and reveals what good and what very bad things can be done with our tongue. He expresses this in chapter 3 of his epistle. In verse 2 he begins by talking about the offenses we all do. Obviously, offenses are done in many ways, but we usually offend with our words. Then he speaks of the power of the tongue, which "like a rudder is capable of moving a ship: the tongue is a little member, and boasteth great things" (James 3:4–5), and adds, "And the tongue is a fire, a world of iniquity: so is the tongue among our members, that it defileth the whole body, and setteth on fire the course of nature; and it is set on fire of hell" (James 3:6).

The tongue is a world of evil, it is a member of ours that can have a direct connection to hell itself. He also adds, "But the tongue can no man tame; it is an unruly evil, full of deadly poison" (James 3:8).

Finally, he closes his dissertation by mentioning that we cannot bless God with it and curse men. He compares it like trying to draw sweet and bitter water from the same source (James 3:9–11).

Just so that we have an idea of what we are talking about, the Bible provides a list of sins of the tongue, which must be left behind, if anyone wants to live a holy life. The following are examples of what comes from the misuse of the tongue.

- Speak corrupt words – Ephesians 4:29.
- Anger, rage, screaming, slander and malice – Ephesians 4:31.
- Indecent words – Colossians 3:8.
- Blasphemy and insulting words – 1 Timothy 6:4.
- Gossip – Proverbs 16: 28 and 18:8; 1 Timothy 5:13.
- Murmur – 1 Corinthians 10:10.
- Lying – Ephesians 4:25.

4.   The Holiness of Our Flesh

Finally, we must mention that everything we think and feel deep in our hearts and minds must manifest itself externally. Although this point will be discussed later, it is advisable to close this subsection with the analysis of the works of the flesh, which come from an unsanctified heart. Paul says, "Now the works of the flesh are manifest, which are these; Adultery, fornication, uncleanness, lasciviousness, Idolatry, witchcraft, hatred, variance, emulations, wrath, strife, seditions, heresies, Envying, murders, drunkenness, reveling, and such like: of the which I tell you before, as I have also told you in time past, that they which do such things shall not inherit the kingdom of God" (Galatians 5:19–21).

We should note that "the flesh" in this context refers to disorderly passions, which begin in the heart and are carried out in our members. It is interesting to note that this passage ends with a strong condemnation to all practitioners of these works of the flesh, for "they will not inherit the kingdom of God". Therefore, we are exhorted to live in holiness.

We finish this subsection by emphasizing that inner holiness deals with many matters that pertain our inner being, which is why it is vitally important that we pay attention so as not to resemble the scribes and Pharisees who lived a false and hypocritical holiness.

Outer Holiness

The Church of Christ believes and must live in holiness, not only because the Bible teaches it, but because it is a demand of God, as we have already mentioned in previous chapters. God wants His people to be holy, and that holiness is reflected through our actions and our behavior. That is why this chapter is dedicated to points that are oftentimes not given importance, especially in a society like the one we live in today.

The Importance of External Holiness

Many people think and say that God only cares about the heart and that He does not care how we look on the outside, however, that is a great mistake. Jesus did care about outer holiness when He said, "Thou blind Pharisee, cleanse first that which is within the cup and platter, that the outside of them may be clean also" (Matthew 23:26).

Christ makes His position clear regarding what is seen outside the individual, for what is seen on the outside represents what is inside. He says, "For out of the abundance of the heart the mouth speaketh. A good man out of the good treasure of the heart bringeth forth good things: and an evil man out of the evil treasure bringeth forth evil things" (Matthew 12:34–35).

So, if a person has a holy and pure inner life, they will also reflect it on the outside in every way.

The Practice of External Holiness

One of the clearest forms on the practice of external holiness is manifested by the way we dress, speak, comb our hair, and the way we behave before society. As children of God, we are the light of the world and must bear a good testimony. Clothes do not make a Christian, but Christians reveal their identity through their clothes and appearance (Bacchiocchi).[50]

God's Rules of Dress

1.   The Priest's Wardrobe

When God called Israel His people, He also gave them rules that they should follow. When He called His priests, He also gave them rules that they should abide by. The priest did not wear just any clothing, he had to dress according to what God had established because his garment was sacred. God had told Moses, "And thou shalt make holy garments for Aaron thy brother for glory and for beauty" (Exodus 28.2-36).

The priest's garment was full of typology, every detail had been considered and dictated by God. If God didn't care how His children dressed, He wouldn't have established it, but He cares about this subject, and if God cares, we must care too.

2.   Men's and Women's Clothing

For God there is a clear vision of how both man and woman should dress and has made it well established since ancient times. Each person must dress appropriately and respect their gender, as God made it very clear. "The woman shall not wear that which pertaineth unto a man, neither shall a man put on a woman's garment: for all that do so are abomination unto the Lord thy God" (Deuteronomy 22:5).

---

[50] Samuele Bacchiocchi, Ph.D., *Vestimenta y Ornamentos en el Nuevo Testamento*, Andrews University. en: http://www.laicos.org/sbvestimentantcap3.htm.

At that time, the main garments were the inner robe, which was very tight to the body, and an outer mantle, which was used by men and women (Job 30:18; Songs of Solomon 5:3; and Genesis 37:3). Sometimes, a belt, a coat (for rain) and sandals (Isaiah 3:24; Matthew 5:40) were added. The women also wore a veil, which was the garment that most distinguished them from men when it came to wardrobes. Other garments that made men different from women were the phylacteries, which were worn only by men. For women to be dressed as warriors was not correct (Mattew Henry). How then can we distinguish the clothing between a man and a woman? It is traditionally recognized that men should wear trousers and women should wear a skirt. Although this issue may be different in some religious traditions, the custom for many years has been like this.

Rules for Dress

What should the clothing look like? It is important to highlight the way the Christian must dress to give a good image of who they are. To teach us about this, the Apostle Paul speaks of this in his letter to Timothy and says, "In like manner also, that women adorn themselves in modest apparel, with shamefacedness and sobriety; not with broided hair, or gold, or pearls, or costly array; But (which becometh women professing godliness) with good works" (1 Timothy 2:9–10).

From these verses we can acquire some words that show us how a Christian should dress. These words are decorum, not seductive or provocative, and modesty. However, although this text refers to women, this does not mean that the word does not apply to men.

Decorous Clothing. The word decorum, means, honor, respect, and reverence. The Christian woman's clothing must indicate honor, respect, and reverence. Christians should dress well and elegantly according to their possibilities, for being a Christian should not be a symbol of carelessness, they should not cause pity.

Not Seductive. The word in Spanish is "pudor" (not provocative, seductive, or sexy) means "feeling of reservation towards what may have to do with sex". This means that when the woman or man dresses like this, they usually consider that their clothing is unrelated to sex, that is, that the sexual body parts are not revealed. The same rule applies to males, as there is no distinction between them.

On modesty. The word modesty means it is simple, not luxurious. This is another point that must considered is elegance, it cannot go to the other side of the extreme. Christians are to use modesty every time they dress and not spend a fortune on clothing.

On nudity. The other point that should be considered is nudity because the 21st century is causing a strong influence on society. God has been very strict in the matter of nudity and does not want His children to show their nudity to anyone except their partner. Remember that Ham's sin was seeing his father naked (Genesis 9:22–27).

We must also add that God had certain rules so that nudity would not be discovered. For example, there is a verse that says, "Neither shalt thou go up by steps unto mine altar, that thy nakedness be not discovered thereon" (Exodus 20:26).

This is a clear affirmation that God has been strict in that His children do not show their nakedness. In fact, there is a whole chapter in Leviticus 18 in which God forbids his people to show or uncover the nudity of the father, mother, brothers, cousins, etc.

The Bible affirms that our body is holy and is a temple of the Holy Spirit (1 Corinthians 6:19). You must care for it, and you should not show its nudity. Here, nudity is interpreted as those parts of our bodies that are private and that may have sexual implications, for example, the legs, the breasts, the belly and of course the intimate parts. The Christian must be conservative about this.

Head Cover

One point of great importance pertaining to holiness is concerning the practice of covering or not covering your head when praying. The Biblical passage reads, "Every man praying or prophesying, having his head covered, dishonoureth his head. But every woman that prayeth or prophesieth with her head uncovered dishonoureth her head: for that is even all one as if she were shaven" (1 Corinthians 11:4–5).

Although this is a point that can create some difference between one church and another, the truth is that it is found in the scriptures, and we must pay attention to it. The traditional Christian church teaches that when a woman prays to God or prophesies (speaking of God) she must cover her head, however, if a man prays or prophesies, he must uncover her head. Here are the reasons:

1. Covering is a Matter of Authority

First, verse 3 of Corinthians 11 speaks of the order of authority that exists: God-Christ-Man (husband)-Woman (wife). So, the context of this biblical passage is "authority". Second, it tells us about not affronting the head (the authority). The word affront means shame and dishonor.

Verse 4 adds; "Every man praying or prophesying, having his head covered, dishonoureth his head," (Christ is the head of the man). Verse 5, "But every woman who prays or prophesies with her head uncovered, disgraces her head, for it would be as if she had shaved." (The man is the head of the woman).

In these first two verses we are shown that the male who prays with his head covered, affronts his head, which is Christ; and that the woman who prays with her head uncovered, affronts her authority, which is the male. Here, we find the first reason why the woman covers her head, as a demonstration of being submissive, in this case to her husband and if she is a maiden, to Christ.

2. Covering is Having Respect and a Sign of Authority

Verse 7 speaks of the glory of the man and of the glory of the woman, in which each one respects their glory and is submissive to that glory. Verse 10 reads, "Therefore, (this which is that glory) the woman must have a sign of authority over her head, because of the angels."

This verse indicates that when the woman is praying or prophesying before God, the angels are looking at her too, and as the woman is before God, they realize by the cover of the head whether she is a submissive woman or not.

3.   In the Case of the "Veil"

As for the matter that is sometimes present in verse 15, where it says, "because instead of a veil she is given her hair". Here it is referring to the veil the woman wore on her back and chest. The word veil comes from the Greek word perobolain and means thrown around one. While the veil of the head is called a covering (kata) and covered katakalupto. Not to cover oneself is akatakalupto, uncovered. Therefore, when the Christian woman lets her hair grow, then the long hair does the work of the "perobolain".[51]

Makeup and Jewelry

Should Christians paint themselves, or wear makeup? This is another stone in the shoe for someone who wants to live a Christian life without many restrictions. The truth is, although there aren't many Biblical references to ban it, there aren't any references to not ban it either. It is based on this position that the following conclusions are reached regarding the use of makeup.

1.   Women should not paint themselves.

Painting the face is not recommended for Christian women because this represents a clear dissatisfaction with the way God made them. The

---

[51]   W. E. Vine, Loc. Cit.

woman who paints her face does so because she is dissatisfied with what she looks like, and it is a clear example of vanity.

The Bible mentions a unique case of a woman who painted her face to impress King Jehu (2 of Kings 9:30–37), but that cost her death, for trying to seduce the king. The activity of this evil woman is mentioned in the book of Revelation as a doctrine of seduction (Revelation 2:20).

Nature itself teaches us that the woman is beautiful as God made her and that she does not need to paint her face to look good, let alone to look beautiful. Painting your face is a sign of personal insecurity and dissatisfaction.

2.   Women should not wear jewelry.

Just like makeup is associated with vanity, so are outer adornments (jewelry and flashy apparel). The Christian church teaches that it is not necessary to wear gold, or such garments, because they are not necessary for the children of God.

This was preached by Peter. "Whose adorning let it not be that outward adorning of plaiting the hair, and of wearing of gold, or of putting on of apparel" (1 Peter 3:1–5). Here we can see that the Christian "dress" should not include ostentatious hairstyles, ornaments, and luxurious dresses. It was also preached by Paul. "In like manner also, that women adorn themselves in modest apparel, with shamefacedness and sobriety; not with braided hair, or gold, or pearls, or costly array" (1 Timothy 2:9–10).

Both apostles emphasize the same: Christians should not wear outer ornaments. In this case, the watch cannot be considered as jewelry, as it serves the purpose of giving the time.

Haircut and Hairstyle

The man must cut his hair and the woman must let hers grow. This is what the biblical text teaches us, "Doth not even nature itself teach you, that, if a man has long hair, it is a shame unto him? But if a woman has long hair, it is a glory to her" (1 Corinthians 11:14–15).

It is important to mention that this has also been confused many times because (according to critics) the Bible is not clear in reference to this discipline. One important thing to know, however, is that when the Bible does not elaborate on a topic, it is because the Church was not struggling with that situation, or the issue simply didn't exist at the time. It was very normal for the man to cut his hair and the woman to let hers grow.

In the case of a haircut, some people also argue that some men in the Bible let their hair grow, like Samson (Judges 13:5) who did not cut his hair until he was seduced by Delilah who convinced him to do so, (Judges 16:17). It is necessary to clarify that this has nothing to do with what we are talking about, since Samson and others, including Christ, were Nazarites. That is, people dedicated to God from the womb of their mothers. They should not cut their hair for the duration of the Nazareat (Numbers 6:5). However, by the end of that period they could inevitably shave.

In Christianity, men are required to cut their hair and the woman to let it grow as this represents an honor for each. To do the opposite makes it dishonorable. On the other hand, long hair is considered the most marked difference between a man and a woman. This was the distinction of the locusts of Revelation (Revelation 9:8), which had long hair like women.

As for the hairstyle, curiously the Bible advises that our hairstyle should not be ostentatious. "Whose adorning let it not be that outward adorning of plaiting the hair, and of wearing of gold, or of putting on of apparel" (1 Peter 3:3). The word "ostentatious" means to do something to get attention or for others to look at. God's children must show their difference to the world by the way they behave.

The Engagement Ring

What about the marriage engagement ring? This is another issue that raises a lot of controversy, as there are churches that have a problem with this, and others do not. The ring must be classified within the "golden ornaments" and we do not believe it is necessary to show that we are engaged. Our conduct and respect demonstrate who we are, for many can commit adultery even with the ring on and they do not take it off.

Many argue that society teaches that the wedding ring is the sign that distinguishes those who are married from those who are not. However, we should know that although society has established it as normal, history and the Bible discard it, for there is not a single verse in the Bible where the ring has a relationship with marriage. The Bible speaks of marital gifts, which were usually gold, silver, or other objects, (Exodus 22:17), but they did not include rings.

Relationships with the Unconverted

Another issue pertaining to holiness concerns the loving relationships of converted people with those who are unconverted. The Bible teaches us, "Be ye not unequally yoked together with unbelievers: for what fellowship hath righteousness with unrighteousness? and what communion hath light with darkness?" (2 Corinthians 6:14).

In this verse it is well established that not only the courtship, but the even marriage itself, with people who do not belong to the Christian circle, since they are unconverted, is not allowed. But this is nothing new, for God had made it very clear to His people of Israel, "And when the Lord thy God shall deliver them before thee; thou shalt smite them, and utterly destroy them; thou shalt make no covenant with them, nor shew mercy unto them: Neither shalt thou make marriages with them;

thy daughter thou shalt not give unto his son, nor his daughter shalt thou take unto thy son. For they will turn away thy son from following me, that they may serve other gods" (Deuteronomy 7:1–4). In the same passage God gives the reasons why these kinds of relationships should not be allowed, because they will mislead or separate the children of God.

Relationships with unconverted people were one of the main problems that many men of God and even the people of Israel themselves had. Just look in the book of Judges to see that the people of Israel took from the daughters of the Canaanites, Hittites, Amorites, Perizzites, and Jebusites and gave their daughters to their sons and served their gods, (Judges 3:5–6). In other words, they did the opposite of what God had told them. One of the most famous examples was undoubtedly Samson's. The cause of Samson's fall was the relationship he had with women who were not of God's people and how Delilah, the Philistine pushed that fall. (Judges 14-16).

Conclusion

We conclude the subject of holiness by establishing that our God is very jealous of His children and that He is a holy God. Therefore, all those who desire to follow and serve Him must be holy like Him, for that is His will. We understand that sometimes it is difficult because the world is very striking and even attractive, yet God's reward for staying pure and without blemish in this world is eternal life.

Chapter 14

Tithes, Offerings, and First Fruits

≈

*Bring ye all the tithes into the storehouse, that there may be meat
in mine house, and prove me now herewith, saith the Lord of hosts,
if I will not open you the windows of heaven, and pour you out
a blessing, that there shall not be room enough to receive it.*

MALACHI 3:10

God has established an economic system through which the faith of
every Christian is tested, and their work here on earth is maintained.
This system is based on tithes, offerings, and first fruits. This is one
of the means used from the beginning when God began dealing with
mankind and it continues to be the main source of the church's resources.
In this chapter we will explore the doctrine of this topic, the practice of
the church, and some practical advising.

Tithes and Offerings

Without a doubt, we understand that God has a financial plan to
evangelize the world, and this plan is biblical and consists of each
member of Christ's body fulfilling an obligation to pay tithes and bring
offerings to the storehouse. It is therefore necessary to establish that
tithes represent 10% of all our income and that offerings are "gifts" that
we give to God for what He has blessed us with.

God Commands Us to Pay Tithes

From very early on in Biblical history, God required His children to set aside for Him the tithes of all their income. One of the key verses was given under the law, "And all the tithe of the land, whether of the seed of the land, or of the fruit of the tree, is the Lord's: it is holy unto the Lord" (Leviticus 27:30).

We can observe that in this verse, God asks for tithes of all that was acquired from the earth. Another Bible passage also reads, "Thou shalt truly tithe all the increase of thy seed, that the field bringeth forth year by year" (Deuteronomy 14:22). With this we can see that tithing was established by God as a commandment which should be obeyed.

Tithing was a Common Biblical Practice

Some argue that tithing is something that should not be practiced because it was something that God established under the law, and we are no longer under the law but under grace.

However, it is necessary to emphasize that tithes began to be paid long before the law and has been a normal practice of those who belong to God. In the Bible we can find several examples of people who gave their tithes, since that was the normal practice.

1. Abraham was one of the first to pay tithes on everything he had obtained (Genesis 14:20).
2. Jacob promised God that he would give tithes all that God gave him (Genesis 28:22).
3. The people of Israel paid tithes from the time they were established as God's people, and they held this practice in high esteem (Deuteronomy 12:11 and Leviticus 27:30–32).

God Also Asks for Our Offerings

Apart from the tithes, God asked His people to bring him a voluntary offering. "Speak unto the children of Israel, that they bring me an offering: of every man that giveth it willingly with his heart ye shall take my offering" (Exodus 25:1–2).

Offerings are gifts that God's children give to their Lord for all that God does for them, and they also represent a grateful heart.

The offerings that God's people gave in those days varied in both quantity and variety. That is, the people brought to God what they had received and offered it to God in a certain way (Leviticus 2). There were also different kinds of offerings given to God. For example, peace offerings (Leviticus 3), sin offerings (Leviticus 4), and atoning offerings (Leviticus 5), among others.

The Purpose of Tithes and Offerings

When we study about offerings, we ask ourselves, "Does God need our money?" No! God does not need our money, because He owns the silver and gold of this world (Haggai 2:8). However, God does everything with a purpose and if He established a system of offerings and tithes, it is because He had a plan to do so. Here are some of the purposes for why God established this economic system.

In the Old Testament

1. To help the poor.

God had established a way for the Israelites to help others, but especially the poor and needy. An example of this was the harvest of each sabbatical year since it was reserved for the poor (Exodus 23:11 and Deuteronomy 15:11).

2. For the support of the priests.

Tithes were also used for the priesthood of God's people, who were an entire tribe (Levi), which had been called to devote themselves to the service of worshiping God and ministering to the people. To these, God had not given them an inheritance like the other tribes, and could only live off of what the rest of the people offered and tithed. "And, behold, I have given the children of Levi all the tenth in Israel for an inheritance, for their service which they serve, even the service of the tabernacle of the congregation" (Numbers 18:21).

From this biblical principle arises the idea that tithes serve for the support of all those who are engaged in the service of God, especially ministers.

3. To help the stranger, the orphan, and the widow.

God had provided for the most vulnerable in society at the time: the foreigner, the orphan, and the widow. One of the clearest passages regarding this is found in Deuteronomy: "At the end of three years thou shalt bring forth all the tithe of thine increase the same year, and shalt lay it up within thy gates: And the Levite, (because he hath no part nor inheritance with thee,) and the stranger, and the fatherless, and the widow, which are within thy gates, shall come, and shall eat and be satisfied; that the Lord thy God may bless thee in all the work of thine hand which thou doest" (Deuteronomy 14:28–29 and Deuteronomy 26:13).

This passage speaks to us about the purpose of money in God's plans, which generally served to help all those who did not have any. A widow, for example, had been left without support. A foreigner had left their country and was now away from home and without resources, and would therefore need help. God will always provide for those who need it most.

In the New Testament

Tithes and offerings served to help those in need in the church. That was the practice of the first church, and they did it systematically. "Neither was there any among them that lacked: and distribution was made unto every man according as he had need" (Acts 4:34–35).

Churches also collected additional offerings to meet the needs of God's work elsewhere. "For it hath pleased them of Macedonia and Achaia to make a certain contribution for the poor saints which are at Jerusalem" (Romans 15:26).

In addition to the above, offerings have served in the Old Testament to sustain the teachers and preachers of the church. On this, the Apostle Paul said, "Let him who is taught the word share in all good things with him who teaches" (Galatians 6:6).

In the case of those who were devoted entirely to the ministry of preaching and teaching, including the pastors, Paul says, "Even so hath the Lord ordained that they which preach the gospel should live of the gospel" (1 Corinthians 9:14).

When the Apostle Paul went out on his missionary journeys to preach the gospel, he was sustained by the church of the Philippians (Philippians 4:15–18). For that reason, God blessed them and gave them a promise, "But my God shall supply all your need according to his riches in glory by Christ Jesus" (Philippians 4:19).

Christians should know that each time they give, their contributions are used wisely to cover the necessary expenses of God's work. From this money, pastors are sustained, the needy are helped, and above all, the church's expenses are paid.

The Blessing and Privilege of Giving Tithes

When we talk about tithes and offerings, we must think that it is a privilege that God gives us and a blessing that we can participate in. However, there are times when believers don't do it and end up stealing from what belongs to God.

In the Bible we have the example of the nation of Israel and how God rebuked them harshly because they were stealing from the Lord. "Will a man rob God? Yet ye have robbed me. But ye say, wherein have we robbed thee? In tithes and offerings. Ye are cursed with a curse: for ye have robbed me, even this whole nation" (Malachi 3:8–9).

Although this Biblical passage is very strong, God does not play with His commandments and laws and His children must obey them. Therefore, because money touches on some human weaknesses, we have to consider a few things about it.

Tithing is a Privilege

We know from the word of God that tithing is a great privilege and that it must not be a burden or problem. King David said, "But who am I, and what is my people, that we should be able to offer so willingly after this sort? for all things come of thee, and of thine own have we given thee" (1 Chronicles 29:14). We must recognize that if we have something, it comes from God and that giving to God from what He gives us, is a privilege.

The Blessing of Tithing

When the believer tithes, he/she is put under God's blessing. Then, when the child of God is under God's blessing, God opens the windows of heaven and rebukes the devourer. (Read Malachi 3:10–11). To understand how this works consider the following: Opening the windows means being under divine favor. When a person is under divine favor, everything will work in their favor. For example, their salary at work increases, or when they go to buy something they oftentimes find it cheaper. In other words, God moves His grace in favor of that person so that money will yield more.

The second blessing that follows when the believer tithes, God rebukes the devourer. Rebuking the devourer means being protected. God said that He would rebuke the devourer to not destroy the fruit of the earth and for the earth to produce (Malachi 3:11). This means that God will bring protection over the goods of His children.

When we talk about the devourer described in this text, we ask ourselves, "Who is this devourer?" The devil is described as many things, for example, in the garden of Eden he was a serpent and here, he is described as "the devourer" – which can also be compared to locust (according to the NVI),[52] caterpillar, cicada, grasshoppers, etc. What was the job of a devourer? Usually, the devourer ate the fruit produced from the field, destroyed crops, and ate the fruits (Malachi 3:11).

When a Christian is faithful to God, God will be in charge of rebuking all those who tend to devour their blessings. God will deliver you from thieves and wicked men who want to take away God's blessings.

We must also emphasize that God has promised to prosper His children, but every promise of God also has its conditions. Each condition expressed in the Bible implies an act of obedience. As all obedience implies blessing, the blessing then follows obedience, (Deuteronomy 11:26–28). Here, the promise is "blessing until it overflows" and the condition is to give the tithes to the Lord. We should note that this is the only time in the Bible that God says, "try me on this."

---

[52] Nueva Versión Internacional de la Biblia.

The Curse of Not Tithing

On the other hand, and contrary to the above, not tithing brings a curse. God said to His people of Israel, "Ye are cursed with a curse: for ye have robbed me, even this whole nation" (Malachi 3:9).

This may be a very strong passage, however, we must know that just as God takes His blessings seriously, He also takes it very seriously when we fail Him. The believer must know that stealing from the Lord brings a curse upon themselves. When a person does not tithe, they are voluntarily puts themselves under the curse of the enemy. That means the windows close, and the devourer is released. If the devourer is released, then the produce and fruits will be eaten and there will be no harvest. Moreover, having the windows closed means not having divine favor over our lives, which translates not only into economic results but also losses.

Something we must learn about this curse is that in Christ we have been blessed with every spiritual blessing (Ephesians 1:3) and cannot be cursed. In other words, by giving ourselves to Christ, the devil no longer has power over us. But as we already know, the devil is seeking out who to devour (1 Peter 5:8) and the only way the devil can touch our finances, is if we open the door to him and give him reason to do so. When the Christian does not tithe, then the devil has a legal right to devour our blessings.

Final considerations

Finally, believers should consider some fundamental truths about tithes.

First, when one decimates what one has received, one is giving to eat spiritually. God said, "Bring ye all the tithes into the storehouse, that there may be meat in mine house" (Malachi 3:10). Tithers should know that by bringing tithes to the storehouse, God is in charge of nourishing them spiritually. If a church cannot even support it's pastor, how then will God feed them?

Second, where should tithes be given? God was clear regarding this because sometimes as humans we tend to want to make our own rules and take our own administrative measures. Anticipating this, God Himself said to Israel, "Then there shall be a place which the Lord your God shall choose to cause his name to dwell there; thither shall ye bring all that I command you; your burnt offerings, and your sacrifices, your tithes, and the heave offering of your hand, and all your choice vows which ye vow unto the Lord" (Deuteronomy 12:11). It is important to mention that our tithes must go to the place where God has us gathered together and nowhere else.

There are people who send their tithes to another country, to another church, or simply give it in benevolence to charity. But the Bible clearly states that tithes must go where we congregate. If someone wants to do a charity work or give to some ministry of benevolence, they can do it, but that must be with other money, not with tithes.

Finally, giving tithes must be by obedience and not by force. No one should feel suffocated because they have to give their tithes to the Lord. Usually someone who is grateful to God will willingly give them, because they have learned that therein lies the blessing.

The First Fruits

If God asks us for tithes and offerings, as children of God we have also learned to give Him our first fruits. We do this because we have learned the blessing of giving God from what we receive of Him. We have learned that giving to God is not only good because we obey His word, but by giving to Him, great blessings are unleashed in our lives. However, the topic of first fruits is often not considered, since unlike tithes, first fruits are also a type of offering given to God. "Honour the Lord with thy substance, and with the first fruits of all thine increase: So shall thy barns be filled with plenty, and thy presses shall burst out with new wine" (Proverbs 3:9–10).

Definition

The word first fruits come from the Hebrew word "bekkur" and means "first fruits of harvest, first fruits". This comes from "bakar" which means "to burst the belly, to give birth." In other words, it means, beginning, better, or main. Its application and meanings are simply "a promise to come". It was also the name given to one of the seven most popular festivals that God's people had in the Old Testament. The first fruits were also a special kind of sacrifice, which included the firstborn of the cattle as well.[53]

The Commandment on the First Fruits

It is important to recognize that the practice of giving God the first fruits already existed before the law, and, in fact, this is humanity's oldest kind of offering. The oldest event was found with Abel in the book of Genesis. "And Abel, he also brought of the firstlings of his flock and of the fat thereof" (Genesis 4:4).

Although the first fruits have been given since ancient times, God establishes this practice as a law for the nation of Israel, and just as tithes and different offerings, they should be brought by the people. One verse reads, "The first of the first fruits of thy land thou shalt bring into the house of the Lord thy God. Thou shalt not seethe a kid in his mother's milk" (Exodus 23:19).

One of the reasons why God asked them for the first fruits is because they were established by God to sustain the Levitical priests and to help them in their ministry. God had not given them an inheritance like the other tribes of Israel, and this offering was the main source of their income, that is why God had established it in His word.

"The priests, the Levites shall have no part nor inheritance with Israel; they shall eat the offerings of the Lord made by fire, and His inheritance

[53] James Strong, *Nueva Concordancia Strong Exhaustiva*, (Miami Florida: Editorial Caribe, 2002).

from them that offer a sacrifice, whether it be ox or sheep; and they shall give unto the priest. The first fruit also of thy corn, of thy wine, and of thine oil, and the first of the fleece of thy sheep, shalt thou give him. For the Lord thy God hath chosen him out of all thy tribes, to stand to minister in the name of the Lord, him and his sons forever" (Deuteronomy 18:1–5).

In addition to these first fruits mentioned at the beginning and end of the first harvest, each Israelite was to bear a basket of all the fruits (Deuteronomy 26:2) such as oil, new wine, and wheat; in short, all of the best (Numbers 18:12–19). The firstborns of the animals were also included, to remember that the Lord had delivered them from slavery in Egypt and given them a rich country.

The Feast of the First Fruits

The first fruits were not a burden for God's people, but quite the contrary, they understood it was a blessing to participate in that event. God had reserved a specific day, and it was taken as a great celebration by the people of God. "And thou shalt observe the feast of weeks, of the first fruits of wheat harvest, and the feast of ingathering at the year's end" (Exodus 34:22).

The Feast of the First Fruits was a celebration of rejoicing, in which the first fruits were presented to the Lord, and it was done in a way that indicated joy and rejoicing. The commandment read as follows, "Speak unto the children of Israel, and say unto them, When ye be come into the land which I give unto you, and shall reap the harvest thereof, then ye shall bring a sheaf of the first fruits of your harvest unto the priest: And he shall wave the sheaf before the Lord, to be accepted for you: on the morrow after the sabbath the priest shall wave it" (Leviticus 23:10–11). So, they participated in this feast with great joy.

There were two ways to present the first fruits offering. The first consisted of presenting before the Lord a sheaf of barley, waved and accompanied by an offering of two tenths of an ephah[54] of fine flour kneaded with oil, and a libation of wine. It was offered on the 16th of the month of Nisan, the second day of the Feast of Unleavened Breads, to initiate the harvest (Exodus 23:19; Leviticus 23:9–14; Numbers 28.:16).[55] The second was seven weeks later and the true feast of the first fruits was celebrated, also called "The Pentecost" or the "Feast of Weeks". This festival ended the first harvest of the year and the gathering of the whole harvest. Together with two loaves of the first fruits which were waved before the Lord, seven lambs, a calf, two rams, and a goat were offered (Leviticus 23:15–20).

The Purpose of First Fruits

The first fruits were a prophetic offering announcing God's future blessing. It is interesting to know that the law of the first fruits was given to Israel when they were still in the desert, and when they had not yet received God's promises. The fact that God asked them for the first fruits of a land they had not yet received and the first fruits of the fruits that they had not yet harvested, teaches us God's plan for blessing His people. These first fruits are a prophetic offering of a blessing to come.

The first fruits reflected a spirit of worship to God. God deserves the first and the best. When we consider this, we see that God deserves the most excellent and this is a symbol of worship to God. For example, when we see the case of Abel's offering, we can find excellence and worship in his sacrifice. "And Abel, he also brought of the firstlings of his flock and of the fat thereof. And the Lord had respect unto Abel

---

[54] An Ephah was an ancient measure of capacity for aggregates or granulated material such as lentils, used in ancient times by the Hebrews and Egyptians. It was equivalent to more than 22 liters in each package.

[55] The name given to the month of Nisan in the Bible is simply "the first month" following in the same way the rest of the months of the Hebrew year in the Torah, the ordinal numbering. It is named for the first time in Exodus: This month will be the beginning of the months; for you this will be the first in the months of the year (Exodus 12.2).

and to his offering: But unto Cain and to his offering he had not respect. And Cain was very wroth, and his countenance fell" (Genesis 4:4–5).

Here we can see that the spirit of this man of God was to worship God and presented Him with the first and best he had. Another case is that of Abraham, who not only gave God the first and the best but he offered God his own and only son. "And he said, Take now thy son, thine only son Isaac, whom thou lovest, and get thee into the land of Moriah; and offer him there for a burnt offering upon one of the mountains which I will tell thee of" (Genesis 22:2).

First fruits represent a matter of faith and trust in God. By giving God the first of what we receive, we are testifying that much more is to come. In other words, the first fruits represent only a small part of how much we will receive. By offering God the first fruits and the best of the fruits, He is recognized as the Lord, as the owner and giver of the fruits of the field. It is all due to His blessing. Having consecrated the first fruits to God, the rest of the goods could then be enjoyed with a clean conscience.

In ancient times there was a process for selecting the first fruits of the grains. Each family would be attentive to the first shoots of the plants, and once they found them, they designated them as first fruits by tying them with a red ribbon around the branch or stem.

The Blessing of Giving the First Fruits

The first fruits unleash God's blessing upon our lives. The Bible says, "Honour the Lord with thy substance, and with the first fruits of all thine increase: So shall thy barns be filled with plenty, and thy presses shall burst out with new wine" (Proverbs 3.9-10).

When we give the first fruits to God, we are showing not only that we believe in Him, but that we have faith and confidence that if He gave us the first fruits of the harvest, He would give us a great and blessed harvest. In Proverbs 3:10, full barns means storage of blessings for many days, and this indicates that God's blessing comes in abundance to such an extent that we can store up for the time of scarcity. Bursting presses filled with new wine mean joy and gladness at having received the Lord's blessing.

Conclusion

We conclude this chapter recognizing that all we have is because God has given it to us, and that all the things we have received are God's blessing. We must give God our tithes, which account for 10% of all our entries. But we must also give Him our offerings, which are gifts of thanks given to our Lord. Finally, we must give God the first fruits, for our God deserves the first and the best, and because they represent a prophetic offering of blessings to come.

Chapter 15

The Church

≈

But ye are a chosen generation, a royal priesthood, an holy nation,
a peculiar people; that ye should shew forth the praises of him
who hath called you out of darkness into his marvelous light.

1 PETER 2:9

Another thing we must learn about the Christian doctrine is the study of the Church since the Church is the one that Jesus came to establish in this world as His people and as one of the instruments for evangelizing humanity. In this chapter we will learn the most basic things about the meaning of the word church and its implications with Christianity.

Definition

The word "church" is a translation of the Greek word ekklesia and is often used to designate any assembly or congregation of people gathered for religious or political purposes. Chafer says the word really means "called out." He adds that in ancient Greece, cities were governed by a purely democratic system in which all the citizens of the people met to decide on matters of mutual interest. As they were "called out" of their ordinary occupations to an assembly in which they could vote, the word came to mean the result of those calls, that is, being appointed by those who met. Hence then the Church is the congregation or assembly of Christians who have left the world to form the people of God.[56]

It is important to note that when we say "church" we are not referring to the building in which we gather, although we often refer to it as the church, however, the "Church" is all those who gather in that place to worship God.

The other thing to consider is that the founder of the church is our Lord Jesus Christ. Christ established the Church, which is His people and belongs to Him (Matthew 16:18), which He bought at a high price. Christ bought it with His precious blood (Romans 5:8).

The Nature of the Church

The Church is the greatest thing that God has established in this world and represents something very close to His heart. That is why it is constituted in a unique and special way, according to the taste and whim of our Lord. Next, we will study what the Church is made of, and why God made it that way.

The Church: The Body of Christ

One of the characteristics that distinguishes the Church from any entity is that the Church is the body of Christ and Christ is the head (Ephesians 1:23; 5:23). This speaks of the great unity between our Lord and his Church, as Christ is the head, it indicates that He is the one who directs it and who governs it.

---

[56] Lewis Sperry Chafer, *Teología Sistemática: La iglesia*, seminario Reina Valera, http://www.seminarioabierto.com/doctrina235.htm. Retrieved November 10, 2015.

The Church: An Organism and an Organization

The main emphasis on the New Testament, as Bancroft points out, is on the Church as an (1) organism, the living union of all true believers in Christ. Another concept is that of a local church or an (2) organized church. It is the body of believers who profess to be Christians and gather in a locality or group of such local assemblies (1 Corinthians 1:2; Galatians 1:2; Philippians 1:1).[57]

The Church: An Institution

As Christians we must know that the Church is also an institution created by our Lord Jesus Christ and composed of all men and women without distinction of nationality, language, color, or customs (Ephesians 4:3–6).

The Purpose and Mission of the Church

The New Testament reveals that the church is God's central purpose in today's age, in contrast to God's purpose for Old Testament individuals and nations. The greatest purpose for the nation of Israel is revealed to be the companionship of believers made up of Jews and Gentiles who are called out of the world and come together in a living union by the baptism of the Spirit, and to fulfill God's will on earth.

The Mission of the Church

The Church certainly has a specific mission which it must openly develop. Bancroft says that the Church's mission is broad, and this consists primarily of bearing witness to the truth, to be a permanent dwelling place for God, to bring glory to God, to build members, to discipline its members, and to evangelize the world.[58]

---

[57] Emery H. Bancroft. *Fundamentos de teología bíblica*, (Grand Rapids, MI, 1977) 372.
[58] Emery H. Bancroft. Op. cit., 380-381.

Descriptive Titles of the Church

The Church receives some titles describing its nature and relationship with Christ. We find these in the Bible, let's look at some of them:

1. The Lord's flock (John 10:14–16). If the Church is a flock, then Jesus is the shepherd.
2. Tillage (farmland) and building of God (1 Corinthians 3:9). If the Church is a farm, then Jesus cultivates it.
3. Temple of God (1 Corinthians 3:16). If the church is a temple, then Jesus inhabits it.
4. The body of Christ (Ephesians 1:22–23). If the Church is a body, then Christ is the head and if he is the head, then he is the one who leads this organization.
5. The bride of Christ (Ephesians 5:21–33). If the Church is the wife, then Christ is the husband (although weddings have not yet taken place) and as a husband he loves and cares for his wife.
6. Column and bastion (ground) of truth (1 Timothy 3:15). If the Church is a column, then Christ is the whole house.

Conditions for Church Entry

As every institution requires some form of entry or membership process, the Church also has a process for those who wish to adhere to it. Lyman mentions in his church history that baptism by immersion was the rite of passage in the early Church. This tells us that there is a form of entry and admission.[59] Therefore, we should consider the following: You must enter through the door.

To belong to the Church, you must first enter through the right door. Although someone can look at many doors, to enter the Church there is only one, and that is Christ. Our Master said, "I am the door: by me if any man enters in, he shall be saved, and shall go in and out, and find pasture." (John 10:9).

---

[59] Jesse L. Hurlbut, *Historia de la iglesia Cristiana*, (Miami, FL Vida, 1999) 41.

At this point it must be considered that no one who claims to be a Christian can enter through another door that has nothing to do with Christ. In fact, no one can be called a Christian if they do not have a relationship with Jesus Christ. Entering through the door means entering by the indications of our Lord Jesus Christ.

Entry requirements must be met.

The second condition for whoever wants to enter must meet the entry requirements. Like with every other institution, it is imperative to meet the requirements that the church has used since Jesus established it.

1. Accept Jesus Christ as your personal savior (Matthew 10:10 and John 6:47). Since it is a Christian church and Christ is the Lord of the Church, then it is necessary to accept Christ as Lord and personal Savior.
2. Repenting of sins (Acts 2:38). To enter the church correctly, it is necessary to die to the world and enter into life with Christ. This means that one must repent of their sins, renounce the things of the world, and follow Christ.
3. Baptism (Mark 16:16). The candidate must be baptized in water and by the Holy Spirit. As previously mentioned, baptism is the door that God has established for anyone who wishes to belong to the Church.

Responsibilities and Privileges of Church Members

Like with any entity, we must know that the Church establishes certain privileges and responsibilities for all those who belong to it. Bishop Fortino organizes a list (described below) in his doctrine treatise. He says we have responsibilities that make us mature, and privileges that make us grow. Privileges and responsibilities are outlined for all baptized members.[60]

---

[60] Juan Fortino, . Op.cit., 52.

Privileges

As children of God and members of the Church, God has given us great privileges that those who do not belong to the Church do not have. A privilege is a right that a person has that allows him to do and participate in things that are commonly reserved for members only. Here we have some privileges:

1. Participate in the worship of the Lord (Ephesians 5:18–20).
2. Participate in the sacrament (1 Corinthians 11:23–34).
3. Receive a specific position or function (1 Corinthians 12).
4. Preach the Word of God (Romans 9:14–16).
5. Be recipients of all promises (2 Peter 1:3–4).
6. Be recipients of spiritual gifts (Romans 12:3–8).
7. Eternal life (Luke 18:29–30).

Responsibilities

Every member of the Church should know that once he or she joins the body of Christ, he or she has certain responsibilities that they must fulfill. This not only makes them an obedient member, but also gives them the rights as a responsible member. Below is a list of the most important responsibilities:

1. Assisting all services (Hebrews 10:23–25).
2. Offering (1 Corinthians 16:2–3).
3. Tithing (Ten percent of our earnings) (Malachi 3:7–12).
4. Keeping their testimony (Titus 2).
5. Defending the doctrine (1 Peter 3:15).
6. Living in holiness (Hebrews 12:14).
7. Obeying and respecting the authorities of the Church (Hebrews 13:1).
8. Being good citizens (Titus 3:1).

Conclusion

We conclude this section reminding all Christians, who are God's people and represent Him here on earth, that it is a very great privilege to belong to the body of Christ. Therefore, we must keep the purity of our calling and meet all the standards and requirements that the Church has determined.

Chapter 16

The Lord's Supper and The Washing of the Feet

≈

And as they were eating, Jesus took bread, and blessed it, and brake it, and gave it to the disciples, and said, Take, eat; this is my body. And he took the cup, and gave thanks, and gave it to them, saying, Drink ye all of it; For this is my blood of the new testament, which is shed for many for the remission of sins.

MATTHEW 26:26–28

The celebration of the Lord's Supper is something very special for the Church and is one of the most special sacraments, after baptism. It is a very spiritual experience, because by participating in it, one is transported and at the same time becomes a participant in the sufferings of Jesus in Calvary. This celebration is so special that one must take the time to participate in it and enjoy it in spirit.

Origin of the Lord's Supper

The Jewish Passover

The Lord's supper is the Christian version of the Jewish Passover which consisted of the sacrifice of a Passover lamb once a year. This was done to remember the salvation of the people of Israel from death in Egypt. It also symbolized the freedom from slavery of more than four hundred years in Egypt (Read Exodus 12:1–14).

Definition

The word Passover comes from "pasca", Greek transcription of the Aramaic term for Passover, from the Hebrew "pesach," meaning to pass over, to set aside. This word arises from when the destructive angel, who had been sent to smite the firstborns of the families of Egypt, literally passed over the houses of those who had smeared the blood of the sacrificial lamb over their doors and side posts, according to what God had commanded His children to do (Exodus 12:1–14). God delivered them in a miraculous way because the firstborns of Israel did not perish that night. For that reason, God established this feast so that they would never forget.

Jesus and the Passover

Jesus celebrated and participated in this Passover all His life and even with His disciples. However, when He was establishing His church, He made a change in the Jewish Passover and established instead as "The Supper of the Lord" as we will see in the point below (Matthew 26:20–21).

Institution of the Lord's Supper

The Bible says that while they ate (namely, the Jewish Passover), Jesus instituted the holy supper or supper of the Lord. "And as they were eating, Jesus took bread, and blessed it, and brake it, and gave it to the disciples, and said, Take, eat; this is my body. And he took the cup, and gave thanks, and gave it to them, saying, Drink ye all of it; For this is my blood of the New Testament, which is shed for many for the remission of sins" (Matthew 26:26–28).

It is necessary to understand that with this action, Jesus is establishing a new covenant.

God had made a covenant with Israel in the wilderness so that He could sanctify them and redeem them from their sins. This covenant consisted of different types of sacrifices for the remission of sins. One such sacrifice was the Passover lamb, or rather, that lamb that was sacrificed on Passover day. This sacrifice was made for the whole nation of Israel, but each family had to sacrifice a lamb and eat it. When Jesus was leaving this Earth and is dining with His disciples, He established a new covenant, but now with the Church.

The new covenant replaces the lamb and the blood.

In the old covenant the blood was shed, the lamb along with bitter herbs was eaten, and a ceremony was performed, so they remembered the salvation that God had given them in Egypt. In the new covenant the lamb and blood are replaced. In the new covenant, the bread we eat symbolizes Christ as the lamb and the wine we drink symbolizes the blood shed by Jesus on Calvary.

The new covenant gave it the name "The Lord's Supper".

After Christ ascended to Heaven, the early church no longer used the term "Passover" but used the term "The Lord's Supper." Hence then the terminology "The Holy Supper" referring not to the Jewish Passover, but to the ceremony that Jesus established as a sign of His new covenant with the Church. Sometimes it is also given the name of communion, or the table of communion.

The Practice of the Lord's Supper

As we have seen before, the Lord's Supper is a sacrament of the church and has a very special meaning for Christians, however, we must stop here a bit and ask some questions. For example, "Why we should participate?" And, "How we should do it?" We will be learning about this essential practice to the Christian world.

Why should the Lord's supper be eaten? While there may be many motivations a child of God might have to partake in the Lord's supper, there are at least four biblical reasons on why we should participate in the Lord's Supper.

1.   We do it to remind ourselves that He died for us.

One of the first reasons for a child of God to participate in this sacrament is to remind ourselves that Christ died for us. The biblical text says, "And when he had given thanks, he broke it, and said, Take, eat: this is my body, which is broken for you: this do in remembrance of me" (1 Corinthians 11:24). "Do this in remembrance of me." Just as the Old Covenant with Israel where God commanded them to celebrate the Passover once a year so that they would remember the deliverance and salvation of Israel from Pharoah, as is the New Covenant. Our Lord Jesus Christ does not want anyone to forget His sacrifice, let alone His own life, which was offered in ransom for us. Human beings usually forget things once they have been resolved, however, Jesus demanded us to celebrate, so that we do not forget.

2.   In obedience to His commandment.

The Bible says, "After the same manner also he took the cup, when he had supped, saying, this cup is the New Testament in my blood: this do ye, as oft as ye drink it, in remembrance of me" (1 Corinthians 11:25). "Do this" is a commandment of Jesus for His church. Generally, if we look at any order or word from Jesus in which He asks us to do something, we must obey, and this is one of those cases. Therefore, we must partake in the supper, out of obedience.

3.   To announce the Lord's death, until He comes.

The third reason we must participate in the supper has to do with prophetic eschatology. In other words, the holy supper is a prophetic message of what will happen in the future. Paul's message to the Corinthians says, "For as often as ye eat this bread, and drink this cup, ye do shew the Lord's death till he come" (1 Corinthians 11:26). Then, every time a Christian participates in the Lord's supper, they are confessing that Christ is to come one day to raise His people. Therefore, it becomes a very powerful prophetic message, for it indicates the faith of the believer that Christ is to return to Earth.

4. To have eternal life.

Faithful followers of Jesus must partake in this ceremony to have eternal life. That doctrine is found in the scriptures and was established by our Lord. Let us look at Jesus's position regarding this. He said, "I am the living bread which came down from heaven: if any man eats of this bread, he shall live forever: and the bread that I will give is my flesh, which I will give for the life of the world. The Jews therefore strove among themselves, saying, How can this man give us his flesh to eat? Then Jesus said unto them, Verily, verily, I say unto you, Except ye eat the flesh of the Son of man, and drink his blood, ye have no life in you. Whosoever eateth my flesh, and drinketh my blood, hath eternal life; and I will raise him up at the last day" (John 6:51–54).

This is a powerful but controversial passage because people began to leave when they heard it and even His disciples found it very strong; however, these words have a very impressive meaning regarding what we have been talking about. In this passage, Jesus demands of His disciples that they must eat His flesh and drink His blood to have eternal life. Obviously, Jesus was not referring to literally or physically eating His meat, for they are not cannibals.

What Jesus is saying is that those who do not partake of the Lord's supper, which consists of His body (bread) and blood (wine) will not be able to have eternal life. He also adds one more important point saying, "and I will resurrect him in the last day," emphasizing that the key to being resurrected and having eternal life hangs from one's communion with Him. This communion is to participate in His supper.

How should we eat the Lord's supper? To answer this question Paul speaks of three things to consider when we partake of the Lord's supper, and we find them in the book of Corinthians (1 Corinthians 11:27–29).

1.   We must eat it worthily (1 Corinthians 11:27).

The first thing one should know when partaking in the Lord's supper is that one must eat it worthily. The word "worthy" translates to, "having the favor of God". Although we recognize that God is the one who makes us worthy by His mercy, the child of God must be kept sinless in this world. The supper is eaten by being worthy, and only sin makes the person unworthy. Therefore, the person must ensure that they are worthy.

2.   We must test ourselves first (1 Corinthians 11:28).

The second thing a Christian should know is that anyone who participates in the Lord's supper must first evaluate themselves and do a self-examination. At least, that's the spirit of Paul's word. Although we must clarify that we are not talking about perfection (for no one is perfect only God), we are referring to that which can hinder you and we know is sin according to the Bible. When someone recognizes that they have committed a sin that makes them unworthy, then they should refrain from participating.

3.   We must discern the body and blood of the Lord Jesus (1 Corinthians 11:29).

Finally, the participant must discern the body and blood of Christ, which are a fundamental part of the sacrament. But what does it mean to discern? This word means to separate and can also be translated to examine. Therefore, every participant in the Lord's Supper should know that this is not just any supper, like going to dinner with the family, or a birthday party, where we can all participate; no, this is the Lord's supper, and one must know that this bread symbolizes the body of Christ who was beat for our sins on the cross of Calvary. In this sense, the Apostle says, "the body and blood must be discerned".

Consequences of Indignant Participation

The other issue that is of equal importance, but is neglected very often, is participating of the supper without knowing what one is doing. It must be contemplated that participating in the Lord's supper without considering what has been presented in the preceding paragraph can have serious consequences.

There are at least three consequences for eating the Lord's supper in an unworthy and inadequate manner, which are specified by the Apostle Paul. "For this cause many are weak and sickly among you, and many sleep. For if we would judge ourselves, we should not be judged. But when we are judged, we are chastened of the Lord, that we should not be condemned with the world" (1 Corinthians 11:30–32).

1. He who eats unworthily shall be blamed on the body and blood of the Lord Jesus.
2. He who eats without discerning, eats and drinks judgment for himself, so those who are not baptized cannot participate.
3. Many get sick, others weaken, and others sleep.

As we have seen at this point, there are serious consequences of unworthily participating in the Lord's supper. Someone may ask, and why this harshness? Well, we must know that is about participating in the sufferings of Christ on the cross of Calvary, and that was not a simple thing, but it was very painful for our Master. Therefore, a high respect should be sought for that sacrifice.

The Washing of the Feet

Another aspect that is also included in the ceremony of the holy supper in some Christian traditions is the washing of the feet. While we recognize that not all churches may participate in this, the teaching of this practice is included in this book to understand the reasons why it is placed in the sacred scriptures. The passage in which this Christian practice is established was carried out precisely during the celebration of the holy supper by our Lord Jesus Christ.

"He (Jesus) riseth from supper and laid aside his garments; and took a towel, and girded himself. After that he poureth water into a bason, and began to wash the disciples' feet, and to wipe them with the towel wherewith he was girded" (John 13:1–5). To understand this topic in depth, it is necessary to consider the following things about the doctrine of the washing of the feet.

The Act of Washing the Feet

The passage from John 13 tells us about one of the most sublime acts performed by our Savior. Here we observe the King of kings, humbling Himself as a servant. After partaking in the sacrament, the Lord practices the washing of the feet.

The Bible teaches us this, and it is for this same reason that the Church practices both in the Lord's supper and in the washing of the feet. The Church is aware of the spiritual meaning and teaching that our Lord Jesus Christ left us through this beautiful example. This practice is not a circumstantial case, nor is it simply a rite or a religious habit, but is part of a Christian doctrine, and it is even a commandment.

When did this event take place?

The washing of the feet took place on the first day of the Passover feast. Before the feast, our Lord rose, after having supper and prepared to wash the feet of the disciples. Let us look at this biblical reference, "He (Jesus) riseth from supper and laid aside his garments; and took a towel, and girded himself. After that he poureth water into a bason, and began to wash the disciples' feet, and to wipe them with the towel wherewith he was girded" (John 13:4–5).

The Doctrinal Institution of the Washing of the Feet

The Christian church firmly believes that the sacrament should be practiced as part of a ceremony of communion and humility. The case of the washing that Jesus practiced lets us see that Jesus wants something more from us in this institution. Here are some observations regarding this doctrine:

First, the washing of feet is not the traditional cleansing. It was the oriental custom to wash the feet, however, the practice was that the servants did it to the superiors; but here Jesus, being the Lord, is the one who does it.

Second, they do it during dinner; that is, dinner is interrupted. Everything was ready: the towel, the water and the bowl, and only the servant was missing. The one who should be served appeared and set the example.

Third, everyone took part in it. Although Peter did not want Jesus to wash his feet, Jesus nevertheless forces him to let himself be washed if he wants to have a part with Him (John 13.8). It is in this very verse that the spiritual meaning of this is established: Those who are clean do not need but to wash their feet (v. 10). This indicates that their feet are the ones that got dirty, so they had to be washed. Symbolic term: by washing their feet, they are cleaning themselves from the world's pollution.

This verse gives us the most clarity. Jesus speaks to him of cleanliness and that they are clean, though not all were (referring to Judas). So, this cleansing is not about the cleansing of the body, but spiritual cleansing. Let us remember what God said to Moses, "And he said, Draw not nigh hither: put off thy shoes from off thy feet, for the place whereon thou standest is holy ground" (Exodus 3:5).

The Meaning and Practice of the Washing of the Feet.

We can see that Jesus's desire in this practice is strictly related to two fundamental things.

First, this act is an act of pure humility. "If I then, your Lord and Master, have washed your feet" (John 13:14). Through this practice we realize that here on Earth we are all equal and there is no rank or category.

Second, the washing of the feet is a practice Jesus commanded to do. "Ye also ought to wash one another's feet. For I have given you an example, that ye should do as I have done to you" (John 13:14–15).

Conclusion

We conclude this chapter by focusing on the fact that God has given us the great privilege of participating in the holy supper and the washing of the feet, since it means that we are in communion with Christ and with our brothers and sisters.

Therefore, as children of God we must yearn for the moment, for it represents a very special time when we gather ourselves spiritually and become sensitive to the sacrifice Christ made for us. In addition, we have learned that we must prepare ourselves spiritually to participate in this sacrament.

Chapter 17

The Rapture of the Church

≈

For the Lord himself shall descend from heaven with a shout,
with the voice of the archangel, and with the trump of God: and
the dead in Christ shall rise first: Then we which are alive and
remain shall be caught up together with them in the clouds, to
meet the Lord in the air: and so shall we ever be with the Lord.

1 THESSALONIANS 4:16–17

The doctrine of the church rapture is central to the faith and hope of the saints. However, there are many Christians who are disconnected from that reality or give little importance to this matter. Therefore, it is necessary to teach the Church on this doctrinal point that we should all handle with ease, since many false teachers and preachers periodically announce the end of the world and the coming of Christ (even giving dates of His coming) but it does not happen. This is why this teaching is much needed; first, so that the believer knows about this important event, and second, so that they may be prepared.

The Doctrine of the Rapture of the Church

Among the many future events that are to take place with regard to the Church, one of the most preached about by the early church was precisely "the rapture of the Church". The early church often used the word "Maranatha" which means "the Lord is coming" to greet us and say goodbye at the daily events that the church had. The reason was simple, they were waiting for Christ's return at any time, that they greeted each other in that way, because perhaps that could be the last time they would look at each other here on Earth. The rapture or rising of the church is one of the most exciting topics we find in the Bible and because it describes what God will do with His church. Although for many this subject is something that is not known, even within the religious world, for the Lord's Church it is a powerful message of hope and faith.

Definition

The rapture of the Church is the raising or transfer of the Lord's church to a special place prepared by Christ in Heaven, and that is to happen soon. It is called rapture, from the Greek term "harpaz" which translates to take. It is also called rapture because of the way it is to be carried out. The term also means to be kidnapped or abducted suddenly. Therefore, and taking into consideration this definition, we can know how God will take His church with Him. However, although the rising of the Church is part of Christ's return to earth, it should not be confused with the Second Coming of Christ, for this last event will take place seven years after the rapture of the Church.[61]

Stances on the Rapture of the Church

It is well known to most Christians and Bible scholars that there are different opinions regarding when the Church will be raised. There are at least three very clear positions which are the most popular among evangelical Christians, and these are:

1. Before the tribulation

---

[61] The difference between the rapture and the Second Coming is that in the rapture of the Church Christ returns for His Church, but doesn't step on the earth, as the Church rises and meets Christ in the clouds. But at the second coming, Christ descends to the earth and sets His feet on the Mount of Olives, precisely where He ascended to the heavens.

2. In the midst of tribulation
3. At the end of the tribulation

Tribulation is the base event for all three positions. Tribulation refers to the period of seven years of trials humanity will experience and where punishments of great proportions to the Earth will be experienced. They will be days when human beings will not want to live because of the judgments that God is to bring to all the inhabitants of the earth who did not serve Him and who allowed themselves to be deceived by the enemy (Matthew 24:25; Revelation 6:16).

The exponent's position on this subject is that the Church will be raptured before the tribulation of those days. The reasons for this doctrine are as follows: a literal method of interpretation of the rapture, a dispensational interpretation of the scriptures, the Church and Israel are two different groups in which God has different plans, and a scriptural basis that supports this stance.

A Doctrine Established by Jesus

In the Bible we have many prophecies that speak to us about this matter and its greatest exponent is our Lord Jesus Christ because when He came to earth, eschatological events were His important preaching points. "Then said he to the multitude that came forth to be baptized of him, O generation of vipers, who hath warned you to flee from the wrath to come?" (Luke 3:7)

If we can observe, Christ preached to them about "the wrath to come" in a clear reference to the tribulation that will be in the future.

Here are five essential points about the doctrine of the rapture of the Church established by Jesus.

1. Jesus promises to return as the bridegroom.

First, we should mention that it is well known that Jesus is the future husband of the Church, and our Master promises that He will return to raise up to the Church with whom He is to marry (Revelation 19:7–9). To establish this position, we can read the following passage from Matthew: "Then shall the kingdom of heaven be likened unto ten virgins, which took their lamps, and went forth to meet the bridegroom" (Matthew 25:1).

In this passage of the 10 virgins, Jesus presents a similarity to what the kingdom of heaven should be like, "similar to ten virgins" who await the bridegroom. In it He speaks of his return as a husband who comes for the bride and exemplifies it with this parable of 10 virgins, five wise (who are ready and prepared) and five foolish (who are not ready); making known to us the condition of the Church – those who wait and those who don't.

2.   Jesus promises to raise us up with Him.

The second point concerns Jesus's promises to His followers, His church. One of them is the following: "And I, if I be lifted up from the earth, will draw all men unto me" (John 12:32).

In this passage He says that if He is lifted up from the earth, He will all draw all with Him. Obviously, Jesus knew that He was going to be lifted, for He had said it many times, however, this was the way of speaking in those days. That is exactly what will happen when Christ comes again, He will raise His Church from the Earth.

3.   Jesus promises a place in heaven.

Another reference point about the rapture are the words of encouragement that Jesus says to His followers. "Let not your heart be troubled: ye believe in God, believe also in me. In my Father's house are many mansions: if it were not so, I would have told you. I go to prepare a place for you" (John 14:1–2).

In this passage Jesus promises a place in his father's house. What is His father's house? Our Master teaches it in the famous prayer saying, "Our father who art in heaven" (Matthew 6:9).

4. Jesus promises to return.

Another important point on this subject is another promise from Jesus to His followers. This has to do with a place to be with Him and the way this event is to be carried out. Jesus says, "And if I go and prepare a place for you, I will come again, and receive you unto myself; that where I am, there ye may be also" (John 14:3). In this verse, Jesus speaks of going to heaven and returning, but not only of coming back, but taking His church and taking it to a place prepared to be with Him.

5. The testimony of the angels.

Finally, when Jesus rose to heaven, two men appeared in white robes. These were the same angels who were at the foot of the empty tomb when Jesus was resurrected, which had said, "Ye men of Galilee, why stand ye gazing up into heaven? this same Jesus, which is taken up from you into heaven, shall so come in like manner as ye have seen him go into heaven" (Acts 1:11). With this very important revelation of the angels, the basis of this doctrine is closed, for in the same way that He rose, so will He descend. Although this part may also refer the descent of Jesus on the Mount of Olives during His Second Coming, these words are said to the followers of Jesus to give them encouragement that Jesus would return.

With these Biblical passages and many more it was prophesied that Jesus would return, but this time to raise up His church and to take her with Him. In this word the Church has always waited. This is our hope and our faith, that He will return for us. If Jesus promised to return, He will fulfill it because He is not a man to lie, nor a son of man to repent.

What is the rapture of the church?

The Rapture Consists of a Transfer

The rapture of the Church consists of a transfer, that is, the Church will be moved from one place to another. This will happen to give rise to God's divine plan for humanity. The rapture is the setting for the great tribulation that will come upon the face of the earth.

There are two words we should consider when we talk about the transfer of the church. The first word is "transfer" from the Greek word metathesis, which means change of position. With this word we can understand that the Church will be changed from a lower position to a higher one. The other word is "transpose" from the Greek word metatithemi, which means to transfer to another place. An example of this word is in the biblical story of Enoch. "By faith Enoch was translated that he should not see death; and was not found, because God had translated him: for before his translation he had this testimony, that he pleased God" (Hebrews 11:5).

Enoch is a clear example of how the Church is to be transposed. This man of God, of whom we know little, except for extra biblical literature, had the great experience of being transferred to heaven while he was alive. That is, God suddenly took him while he was living here in this world and put him in a place in Heaven with God. The Church will also be moved from Earth to Heaven.

By translating these terms can we find the nature of the rapture of the Church and the condition it must be in when the Lord takes it with Him. The church must be elevated, not only in place but in position as well.

The rapture is part of God's judgment.

Another significant point about the rapture is the eschatological repercussions of it. The rapture of the Church is the beginning of God's judgments and punishments for this humanity; but it is also the door for Satan to deceive this world, because, as the Church is raptured, the Holy Spirit will be removed from the earth. Of this the Bible says the following, "And now ye know what withholdeth that he might be revealed in his time. For the mystery of iniquity doth already work: only he who now letteth will let, until he be taken out of the way. And then shall that Wicked be revealed, whom the Lord shall consume with the spirit of his mouth and shall destroy with the brightness of his coming" (2 Thessalonians 2:6–8).

This event has some very important points to keep in mind especially regarding the time this event will occur and the place where it will happen. The rising of the church will give way to the open manifestation of the antichrist and the beginning of the enemy's evil plans.

Elements of the Rapture

Christians shall undergo a transformation.

To enter the spiritual world, you must enter the spirit, for the Bible says that flesh and blood cannot enter (1 Corinthians 15:50). For this reason, the Lord must transform our bodies into spiritual and incorruptible bodies, those which can enter the presence of the Lord.

To better explain this, it is necessary to consider the words of the Apostle Paul to the Corinthians. "Behold, I shew you a mystery; We shall not all sleep, but we shall all be changed, In a moment, in the twinkling of an eye, at the last trump: for the trumpet shall sound, and the dead shall be raised incorruptible, and we shall be changed" (1 Corinthians 15:51–52).

In this biblical passage we can find more concise details of how the transfer or transposition of the Church is to take place. The child of God who has remained faithful will be transformed from a corruptible and sinful body into an incorruptible and pure body in the blink of an eye, indicating that it will be in seconds when he/she will be raptured with Christ, just as we will see below.

Christians will receive a heavenly body and garment.

To enter heaven with Christ, the child of God must be dressed in special clothing, which is not earthly and much less physical, it is heavenly.

"For we know that if our earthly house of this tabernacle were dissolved, we have a building of God, a house not made with hands, eternal in the heavens. For in this we groan, earnestly desiring to be clothed upon with our house which is from heaven" 2 Corinthians 5:1–2.

Although this verse can be interpreted symbolically, since heavenly garments allude to what we spoke about above, but this means that the child of God is to receive a heavenly body, since it is humanly impossible to enter Heaven and to see Christ in spirit.

Christians shall be resurrected and lifted into the air.

Finally, if any Christians are dead, they will be resurrected, and will later be carried away and raised in the air to meet Christ. Perhaps this is the greatest thing we can expect Jesus to do with his Church, that if someone died in Christ and is buried, when Christ comes, that person will rise from the grave to be raised with the Lord. But if the believer is alive, then they will receive a transformation and be lifted up together with the others who have risen. Paul's passage regarding this reads as follows, "For the Lord himself shall descend from heaven with a shout, with the voice of the archangel, and with the trump of God: and the dead in Christ shall rise first: Then we which are alive and remain shall be caught up together with them in the clouds, to meet the Lord in the air: and so shall we ever be with the Lord" (1 Thessalonians 4:16–17).

It is quite impressive to know that the child of God has died, they must be resurrected from the dead and then be raised, or if they are alive, then they be transformed into a spiritual body and in the same way, as the previous ones, and be raised in the air to always be with the Lord.

The Position of the Church

Heavenly Citizenship

Among the many blessings that await the faithful Christian is his eternal residency. The greatest thing of all is that we will be citizens of the holy city where God is. The Apostle Paul tells the Philippians, "For our conversation is in heaven; from whence also we look for the Saviour, the Lord Jesus Christ" (Philippians 3:20).

It is to be considered that many have dreamed of that moment and will finally be able to enjoy it, as they walk through those streets and admire the beauty of the New Jerusalem. Then, we Christians will have a new citizenship – we will be citizens of a heavenly city forever. John describes the nature of the city a little saying, "And he carried me away in the spirit to a great and high mountain, and shewed me that great city, the holy Jerusalem, descending out of heaven from God, Having the glory of God: and her light was like unto a stone most precious, even like a jasper stone, clear as crystal" (Revelation 21:10–11).

This great servant of God had the privilege of looking into the future and seeing what the city will be like where all the redeemed are to live forever with the Savior.

An interesting fact is to know is that in that city, "There shall in no wise enter into it anything that defileth, neither whatsoever worketh abomination, or maketh a lie: but they which are written in the Lamb's book of life" (Revelation 21:27).

Therefore, whoever wants to end up in this glorious city must prepare to be able to enter that place. The Bible is quite specific regarding the restrictions that those who wish to be there have.

The church must be waiting for the rapture.

This is why we cannot lose hope, nor can we give up on the fact that the Lord will come, even if some count it is as being late. The Apostle Peter exhorts the Church when he tells them, "The Lord is not slack concerning his promise, as some men count slackness; but is longsuffering to us-ward, not willing that any should perish, but that all should come to repentance" (2 Peter 3:9).

The early Church lived in a constant wait for Christ. Although through the ages there have been many people who have dared to set dates of His coming, no one can really set a date for it, for the Bible says, "Watch therefore: for ye know not what hour your Lord doth come" (Matthew 24:42); and, "Watch therefore, for ye know neither the day nor the hour wherein the Son of man cometh" (Matthew 25:13).

Conclusion

We conclude this chapter by mentioning that the rapture of the Church is imminent (meaning it is going to happen, and no one can prevent it) and we must be prepared for that day. Although no one knows when it will be, one thing we do know is that it will certainly happen. Therefore, we must ensure that it does not catch us off guard (Matthew 24:36–44).

Bibliography

Bacchiocchi, Samuel. Vestimenta y Ornamentos en el Nuevo Testamento, Andrews University. en: http://www.laicos.org/sbvestimentantcap3.htm.

Bancroft, Emery H. Fundamentos de Teología Bíblica. Grand Rapids Michigan: Editorial Portavoz, 1986.

Berkhof, Louis. Teología Sistemática. Jenison, MI: T.E.L.L., 1995

Betancourt, Esdras. Manual de Consejería Pastoral. Cleveland, TN: Editorial Evangélica, 2015.

Comentario Bíblico de Mattew Henry. Traducido y editado por Francisco Lacueva; Barcelona, España: Editorial CLIE, 1999.

Diccionario de Ética cristiana y teología pastoral. Barcelona España: Editorial CLIE, 2004

El Pequeño Larousse Ilustrado. México D.F.: Edición Larousse, 2005

Enciclopedia Electrónica Ilumina. Nashville, TN: Caribe –Betania Editores, 2005

Fortino, Juan. Curso Apostólico de Formación Doctrinal, Miami FL: Departamento de publicaciones, Colegio Apostólico de la Florida, 1997.

Galán, Vicente. Ética del comportamiento cristiano. Barcelona España: Editorial CLIE, 1992.

Geiser, Norman y Brooks, Ron. Apologética, Miami FL: Editorial UNILIT, 1995.

Grenz, Stanley J, David Guretzky y Cherith Fee Nordling. Términos Teológicos. El Paso TX: Editorial Mundo Hispano, 2006.

Grudem, Wayne A. Cómo entender la salvación: Una de las siete partes de la Teología Sistemática. Nashville TN; Zondervan, 2013.

Hodge, Charles. Teología Sistemática. Barcelona España, Editorial CLIE, 1991.

Lacueva, Francisco. Curso de Formación Teológica Evangélica. Barcelona, España: Editorial CLIE, 1975.

Liardon, Roberts. Los Generales de Dios. Buenos. Aires Argentina: Editorial Peniel, 2000.

Lopez, Ediberto. Cómo se formó la Biblia. Minneapolis, MN: Augsburg Fortress, 2006.

Lyman, Jessy H. Historia de la Iglesia Cristiana. Miami FL: Editorial Vida, 1999.

Maier, Paul L. Eusebio Historia de la Iglesia. Gran Rapids MI: Editorial Portavoz, 1999.

Maier, Paul L. Josefo. Las obras esenciales. Grand Rapids MI: Editorial Portavoz, 1994.

Martínez, Juan F. Y Scott, Luis. Iglesias peregrinas en busca de identidad. Buenos Aires Ar: Editorial Kairós, 2004.

Mcdowell, Josh y Bob Hostetler. Es bueno o es malo. El paso TX: Editorial Mundo Hispano, 1996.

McDowell, Josh. Evidencia que exige un veredicto. Deerfield FL: Editorial Vida, 1993.

Munroe, Myles. Entendiendo el propósito y el poder de los hombres. New Kensington, PA: Whitaker House, 2003.

Narramore, Clyde M. Enciclopedia de Problemas sicológicos. Miami, FL: Editorial UNILIT, 1970.

Osborne, Cecil G. Psicología del Matrimonio. Miami, FL: Editorial UNILIT, 1989.

Pentecost, J. Dwight. Eventos del Porvenir, Deerfield FL: Editorial Vida, 1984.

Ramos, Marcos Antonio. Nuevo diccionario de Religiones, Denominaciones y Sectas. Miami, FL: Editorial Caribe, 1998.

Simposio Doctrinal Apostólico, Dallas Texas: Secretaria de Educación Cristiana, 2007

Smalley Gary, El gozo del Amor Comprometido. Tomo 1 y 2, Nashville, TN: Editorial Betania, 1986.

Strong, James, LL.D., S.T.D. Nueva Concordancia Strong Exhaustiva. Nashville, TN: Editorial Caribe, 2002.

Tinoco, Roberto. La deserción en la iglesia: por qué la gente se va y qué podemos hacer. Bloomington IN: WestBow Press, 2016.

Tinoco, Roberto. La vida cristiana: una guía bíblica para nuevos convertidos. Bloomington, IN: WestBow Press, 2016.

Vine, W.E. Diccionario Expositivo de palabras del Antiguo y Nuevo Testamento. Nashville, TN: Grupo Nelson, 2007.

Vine, W.E. Diccionario Expositivo de Palabras del Nuevo Testamento. Barcelona España: Editorial CLIE, 1984.

Printed in the United States
by Baker & Taylor Publisher Services